Let's Get Musical GCSE Workbook

for the Edexcel 9-1 Exam

Chris Gill

Let's Get Musical

GCSE Workbook

for the Edexcel 9-1 Exam

Copyright © 2017 by Chris Gill

First edition: December 2017

ABOUT THE AUTHOR

Chris Gill has a Bachelor of Music from the University of Birmingham and a Postgraduate Certificate of Education in Secondary Music from University College Worcester. He has twenty years' experience in teaching music in both the independent and state sectors, and is currently Director of Music at Rye St Antony, Oxford. He has also worked as a freelance conductor and is the founder and chairman of Heritage Opera.

www.chrisgill.co.uk

Other books by Chris Gill

Let's Get Musical – Year 7 Workbook

Let's Get Musical – Year 8 Workbook

Let's Get Musical – Year 9 Workbook

Let's Get Musical – Years 7-9 Teacher's Guide

Harmonising Bach Chorales

The Heritage Opera Guide

Contents

Preface

This book provides a complete two-year course of study for pupils taking Edexcel 9-1 GCSE Music. As a workbook, there is no need for additional textbooks, exercise books, files, or anthologies: performing, composing and appraising activities are all within these pages.

Pupils are able to analyse all eight set works with the aid of structured listening exercises, and there are plenty of additional exercises for for wider listening. Several complete scores are given for both set works and wider listening.

There is a detailed step-by-step composing project for each area of study to guide pupils through the process of creating music in a methodical way.

Performing opportunities are provided across a range of musical styles, using a variety of notation, from chord charts to full scores.

The book also includes a full glossary, listening records for wider listening, performing and composing assessment forms, and blank manuscript paper.

Chris Gill
Oxford, December 2017

The GCSE Music Course

GCSE Music is for anyone who enjoys making music. You can play any instrument or sing. You do not have to read music, but you will learn some notation along the way. You do not have to have taken any grade examinations, either practical or theory, although they all help. As long as you want to perform, compose, and listen to a range of music, this course is for you.

GCSE Music continues the three musical skills which have been developed throughout Years 7-9: Performing, Composing and Appraising (Listening). As you would expect from a practical subject, two out of the three components (Performing and Composing) are entirely based on controlled assessment (coursework). The only examined component is Appraising, which mostly focuses on eight set works studied throughout the course.

Performing (30%)

During the course, you perform, singing or playing, at least one minute as a solo and at least one minute in an ensemble. The combined length of these performances must be at least four minutes. The performances are recorded by May of Year 11, marked by your music teacher, and moderated externally. The solo and ensemble performances are each marked on Technique, Expression and Interpretation, and Accuracy and Fluency. This raw mark can then be scaled upwards if the demand of the piece is the equivalent of Grade 4 or above.

Composing (30%)

During the course, you compose two compositions which are submitted by May of Year 11. Many students choose a computer notation program software to complete this task. One composition is a free choice and the other is chosen from one of four briefs relating to the areas of study - see Appraising below. You will be guided throughout the composition process by your teacher. There are several step-by-step composing projects included in this book, linked to the areas of study: songwriting, ground bass, blues, and sonatina for piano. You do have to record your compositions, but most computer notation programs will do this for you, to save you having to perform your compositions.

Appraising (40%)

You will learn to describe set works and other pieces by referring about their context, for example Baroque era or Film Music, and musical features, for example melody, rhythm and chords. You will have plenty of practice of the type of questions in the listening examination: mainly short questions about the set works. There is also a short question where you write down a few notes of melody and rhythm which you hear several times and some short questions about an unfamiliar piece of music related to one of the Areas of Study. Finally, you write an extended answer comparing one of the set works with an unfamiliar piece from the same Area of Study.

Overview of Set Works

Listen to excerpts from all of the set works and write your comments below.

Area of Study	Composer/Title	Your comments
1 Instrumental Music 1700–1820	Johann Sebastian Bach: Brandenburg Concerto No. 5 in D major, 3rd movement	
	Ludwig van Beethoven: Piano Sonata No. 8 in C minor, 'Pathétique', 1st movement	
2 Vocal Music	Henry Purcell: 'Music for a While'	
	Queen: 'Killer Queen' from the album *Sheer Heart Attack*	
3 Music for Stage and Screen	Stephen Schwartz: 'Defying Gravity' from *Wicked*	
	John Williams: 'Main Title/Rebel Blockade Runner' from *Star Wars*	
4 Fusions	Afro Celt Sound System: 'Release' from the album Volume 2: Release	
	Esperanza Spalding: 'Samba Em Prelúdio' from the album *Esperanza*	

The Elements of Music

Any piece of music can be fully analysed by breaking it down into the Elements of Music below, which can be remembered with DR T SMITH, which spells the initials of each element:

Dynamics

- From loud (forte) to soft (piano)
- Getting louder (crescendo) – getting softer (diminuendo)

Rhythm

- Semibreve, minim, crotchet, quaver, semiquaver, demisemiquaver
- Dotted rhythms, syncopation, hemiola, cross-rhythms
- Tuplets: duplets, triplets, quadruplets, quintuplets, sextuplets, septuplets, etc.
- Tempo markings: fast (allegro), slow (adagio), beats per minute (bpm) etc.
- Changes of tempo: getting faster (accelerando), getting slower (ritardando/rallentando)

Texture

- Monophonic, homophonic, polyphonic, heterophonic, layered
- Harmonic intervals: unison, octaves etc.

Structure

- Repetition and contrast
- Phrase structure, call-and-response, riff, ostinato
- Binary, ternary, variations, sonata, strophic, popular song forms

Melody

- Melodic shape and range, steps (conjunct) and leaps (disjunct), melodic intervals
- Scales (pentatonic, major, minor, chromatic, modal etc.)

Instrumentation

- Strings, woodwind, brass, percussion, electronic instruments
- Voices: soprano, alto, tenor, bass
- Ensembles: orchestra, jazz group, rock group, choir etc.

Tonality

- Major, minor, chromatic, quartal

Harmony

- Triads, sevenths, extended and altered chords

Music for Stage and Screen

Musical Theatre: Rodgers and Hammerstein

Oklahoma! was the first musical written by Rodgers and Hammerstein, who would go on to create *South Pacific*, *The King and I* and *The Sound of Music*. It was first performed in 1943 on Broadway (New York's theatre district) and has been popular ever since.

Oklahoma! is one of the most important musicals ever written because it revolutionised the genre. Before the Second World War, in the 1920s and 1930s, so-called 'Tin Pan Alley' musicals were mostly light comic plays interspersed with popular songs. *Oklahoma!* skilfully combined drama and music into an integrated art-form which is serious and moving, as well as funny. Rather than interrupting the spoken scenes, the songs grow naturally from the drama and often including sections of spoken or semi-spoken dialogue which progress the drama. Short tunes called 'leitmotifs' are associated with different characters and the emotions they represent.

1. List four musicals written by Rodgers and Hammerstein. [4]

    ....

    ....

    ....

2. Describe the 'Tin Pan Alley' musicals of the 1920s and 1930s. [2]

    ....

    ....

    ....

3. How was *Oklahoma!* different from earlier musicals? [2]

    ....

    ....

    ....

4. What name is given to short tunes associated with characters and emotions? [1]

    ....

Listening to *Oklahoma!*

Watch and listen to some excerpts from the National Theatre production from 1998 starring Hugh Jackman as Curly. A video of the whole (three-hour) production is available on YouTube, as is the cast recording. The timings below refer to the video.

Watch the opening scene (3.22-17.35), in which we meet the cowboy Curly, the farm girl Laurey, her Aunt Eller and the sinister farm hand Jud Fry. This scene includes the first two songs: 'Oh, What a Beautiful Mornin'' and 'The Surrey with the Fringe on Top' (both sung by Curly).

'Oh, What a Beautiful Mornin''

1. What instrument imitates the sound of birdsong before the song begins? .... [1]

2. What word, ending in -phonic, best describes the texture of the first two phrases of the song ('There's a bright golden haze on the meadow')?... [1]

3. How many beats in a bar are there in this song?.............[1]

4. What kind of key is this song in: major or minor? .... [1]

5. What are the names of the TWO different sections in this song (and countless other songs)?

   ………………………….. and ………………………… [2]

6. What happens to the tempo between these two sections?

   ………………………………………….. [2]

7. Describe the structure of the song by writing the two sections in the correct order, repeating them where necessary. [3]

'The Surrey with the Fringe on the Top'

Note: a 'surrey' is a type of horse-drawn carriage.

1. How many beats in a bar are there?.............[1]

2. What kind of key is this song in? .... [1]

3. Each verse of this song uses a 32-bar song form that was very popular in the 'Tin Pan Alley' era of the 1920s and 1930s. The 32 bars split into four sections of eight bars each, one of which is different from the others. Which 8-bar section of each verse is the middle eight: the 1st, 2nd, 3rd or 4th section? ……………………………….. [1]

4. What cadence is used at the end of each verse? .... [1]

5. There are three verses in this song. Describe the dynamics of each verse. [3]

   Verse 1 ………………….. Verse 2 …………………. Verse 3 …………………..

'People Will Say We're Love'

Now watch the duet between Curly and Laurey, 'People Will Say We're Love' (59.52-1.04.24).

    1. How many beats in a bar are there?..............[1]

    2. What kind of key is this song in? ……………………………. [1]

    3. What cadence is used in the second phrase ('Don't please my folks too much)? ……………………….. [1]

    4. Which words begin the middle eight section of the song? ……………………………. [1]

    5. How do the first two notes of the middle eight melody differ from the beginning of the melody? ……………………….. [1]

'Out of My Dreams'/'Dream Ballet'

Finally, watch the song 'Out of My Dreams' and the 'Dream Ballet' sequence at the end of Act I (1.26.26-1.44.57).

Describe the musical features of the ballet, including any leitmotifs you recognise from earlier songs.

....

....

....

....

....

....

....

....

....

More Rodgers and Hammerstein Musicals

After the success of *Oklahoma!* (1943), Rodgers and Hammerstein went on to create several other well-received musicals, all of which were turned into films. Here are some of them below:

Carousel (1945)

The Hungarian setting of the source material (Ferenc Molnár's play *Liliom* from 1909), is moved to Maine, a state on the north east coast of the USA in 1873. Billy Bigelow, who works at a fairground carousel, and Julie Jordan, a millworker, have both lost their jobs. They get married and Julie becomes pregnant. In order to provide for his family, Billy turns to crime, but he is killed in the course of a botched robbery. He is refused entry to heaven until he proves that he can be considerate to others. He goes back to earth and sees his grown-up daughter, Louise, and although she cannot see him, he inspires her to break free of her troubled past and make her own life. Like *Oklahoma!*, *Carousel* uses a ballet sequence; and like *Oklahoma!* it breaks the mould of musical theatre, in this case by presenting an antihero as the main character.

Carousel has many famous tunes, including the Carousel Waltz (which is heard instead of an overture) and the songs 'If I Loved You', 'June is Bustin' Out All Over' and 'You'll Never Walk Alone'. The last of these has become an inspirational song in its own right, especially for Liverpool Football Club.

Performing: You'll Never Walk Alone

The sheet music for this song is widely available. You can sing or play the melody (which has a range of an octave and a half) and/or play the chord sequence, which is in C major.

South Pacific (1949)

This musical is based upon James A. Michener's book *Tales of the South Pacific* (1947), a collection of short stories describing the experience of American navy and other military personnel stationed in the Polynesian islands in the fight against Japan during World War II.

This time it is the anti-racist theme of the musical that is groundbreaking. The main American characters, Nellie Forbush and Joe Cable, are both attracted to people from a different background to their own. Nellie falls in love with Emile de Becque, a French plantation owner, who has two children from his marriage with a Polynesian lady who has since died. When Nellie discovers he has mixed-race children, she breaks off the relationship. Meanwhile, Joe Cable meets a beautiful Polynesian girl called Liat, but refuses to marry her because of his racial prejudice. When Emile and Joe go on a daring mission into enemy territory, Nellie is forced to examine her own prejudices. But Emile is in great danger – has she left it too late to come to her senses?

The musical contains many famous songs, including 'Some Enchanted Evening', 'Younger than Springtime', 'There is Nothing Like a Dame', 'This Nearly Was Mine' and 'I'm Gonna Wash that Man Right Outta My Hair'. Much of the music that is associated with the Polynesians in the story, especially Bloody Mary's songs 'Bali Hai' and 'Happy Talk', have elements of **exoticism** – the influence of Eastern music on Western composition. This is evident in the use of unusual instrumentation and hints of different scales in the melody.

Listening: 'Bali Hai'

Listen to 'Bali Hai' and discuss the exoticism in the music, focussing on instrumentation and melody.

The King and I (1951)

The King and I tells the true story of a British governess, Anna Leonowens, who goes to Siam (now Thailand) in the early 1860s to teach the King's many children. The theme of the musical is about the meeting of two proud people from very different cultures – British and Siamese – and how they gradually grow to respect each other. Once again, Rodgers and Hammerstein present a strong independent-minded female leading character, who holds her own against a strong-willed and very powerful king. Anna particularly disapproves of the fact that the king initially insists that she live in the royal palace, along with his many wives. The sub-plot concerns Tuptim, a Burmese slave who is desperate to escape with her lover; the dance sequence in Act II is a play-within-a-play written by Tuptim and based upon a famous American anti-slavery novel of the time, *Uncle Tom's Cabin*. The musical includes 'I Whistle a Happy Tune', 'Hello, Young Lovers', 'Getting to Know You', 'Something Wonderful', 'I Have Dreamed', and 'Shall We Dance?'.

Listening: 'March of the Siamese Children'

1. Discuss the use of exoticism in the instrumentation and melody.

2. Analyse the structure of the piece:

     a. Use the letters A, B and C to describe the form of the piece. ....

     b. Do you notice any symmetry in the form? ....

     c. Which of these musical forms does it resemble most closely?

     Binary   Ternary   Rondo   Variations

The Sound of Music (1959)

Rodgers and Hammerstein's last musical, was based on the story of the Maria, an Austrian nun who

becomes a governess for the seven children of a retired Navy captain, Georg von Trapp. Over time, they fall in love and marry; but then are forced to flee Austria after the Nazi occupation. There are many famous songs in this musical: 'Do-Re-Mi', 'My Favorite Things', 'Climb Ev'ry Mountain', 'So Long, Farewell', 'Sixteen Going on Seventeen', and 'Edelweiss', which was the last song that Rodgers and Hammerstein wrote together. Both the lyrics and the music for the songs 'I Have Confidence' and 'Something Good' were written by Richard Rodgers for the hugely successful 1965 film, as Oscar Hammerstein had died five years earlier.

Performing: 'Do-Re-Mi'

Learn to sing this song – it is a good way of remembering the 'sol-fa' system of naming the notes in a scale. These note-names are used widely in Europe and are useful for working out degrees of the scale in different keys.

Bernstein: West Side Story

West Side Story is a musical composed by Leonard Bernstein in 1957. It is based on Shakespeare's tragedy *Romeo and Juliet*. There are two rival gangs: the Jets (who are white Americans) and the Sharks (Puerto Ricans who are recently immigrants in America).

Listening: Prologue

Watch the prologue to *West Side Story* and listen to how the simmering tension between the two gangs erupts into a fully-blown street fight.

How does Bernstein create the tension in the music? Think about melody, rhythm, tempo, dynamics, instrumentation and any other musical elements that you think are relevant.

....

....

Listening: Jet Song

The music for the Jets is influenced by jazz, which was popular among young white Americans in the 1950s). What jazz influences can you hear in this song?

....

....

Listening: Something's Coming

Tony used to lead the Jets with Riff, but now wants to leave the gang. He already has a regular job working at the local convenience store.

How does Bernstein create a sense of anticipation in this song?

....

....

Listening: The Dance at the Gym

The music for the Sharks influenced by Latin music (e.g. mambo).

Discuss the jazz and Latin influences in these dances.

....

....

....

Jacobs & Casey: Grease

The lyricist Jim Jacobs and the composer Warren Casey wrote the musical *Grease* in 1971. The plot deals with the intertwining lives of two 'gangs' at Rydell High School: the all-male 'T-Birds', and the all-female 'Pink Ladies'. Sandy is a naïve new student who unwittingly starts at the same school as Danny, leader of the T-Birds, with whom she had a fling over the summer. She is soon befriended by the Pink Ladies – but is she prepared to adapt to their lifestyle – and will she get back together with Danny?

The hugely popular 1978 film version, starring John Travolta and Olivia Newton John, introduced some more contemporary musical styles, like the disco-inspired title song 'Grease (is the Word)', the ballad 'Hopelessly Devoted to You' and 'You're the One that I Want'. However, the musical numbers of the original theatre piece reflect the popularity of rock 'n' roll in the late 1950s setting of the story. Here are some examples to listen to and perform, together with YouTube links from *Grease Live* (2016). The lyrics can be found at https://lyrics.az/soundtracks/grease-live/.

12-bar blues: Greased Lightning

(https://www.youtube.com/watch?v=ZBzFq3M291U&index=2&list=RD_pnL1quIayA)

'Greased Lightning' uses only three chords: C, F and G. The chorus uses the standard 12-bar blues chord sequence and the verse repeats bars 9 and 10, to extend the chord sequence by two bars.

Listen to the song and complete the chord sequences below. Then try performing the song.

CHORUS
Standard 12-bar blues in C

1	2	3	4
5	6	7	8
9	10	11	12

VERSE
Standard 12-bar blues in C
with bars 9-10 repeated

1	2	3	4		
5	6	7	8		
9	10	11	12	13	14

I-vi-IV-V progression

This common chord sequence is so strongly associated with popular music of the time that it is sometimes called the 50s progression (or the ice-cream changes). The chord sequence is even described in the lyrics of 'Those Magic Changes', one of the songs that uses the progression. It is also used in 'Rock 'n' Roll is Here to Stay' (not written for 'Grease', but used to add authenticity: it was a hit song for Danny and the Juniors in 1958) and the final song of the show, 'We Go Together'. Listen to the three songs and complete the I-vi-IV-V progression in the different keys:

Those Magic Changes
https://youtu.be/_pnL1quIayA
C major

Rock 'n' Roll is Here to Stay
https://youtu.be/d1QgI-q4LRA
G major

We Go Together
https://youtu.be/AqAwtTk7HUQ
D major

Lloyd Webber: Joseph and the Amazing Technicolor Dreamcoat

Joseph and the Amazing Technicolor Dreamcoat was composed in 1968 by 19-year-old Andrew Lloyd Webber to lyrics by Tim Rice, for Colet Court School, London. It tells the rags-to-riches story of sibling rivalry and redemption from Book of Genesis (Chapters 37-46). *Joseph* was originally a 15-minute **cantata** (unstaged piece for choir and soloists in several movements, usually based on a religious text), but as it was performed more and more over the next few years, it grew into a full-length musical, and launched the phenomonenally successful career of Andrew Lloyd Webber, who went on to compose *Jesus Christ Superstar* (1970), *Evita* (1976), *Cats* (1981), *Starlight Express* (1984), and *The Phantom of the Opera* (1986).

Joseph and the Amazing Technicolor Dreamcoat contains many songs in an accessible soft-rock style, such as 'Jacob & Sons/Joseph's Coat', 'Any Dream Will Do', and 'Close Every Door'. However, the musical also showcases Lloyd Webber's talent for **pastiche** (where a piece consciously imitates a particular style of music), like 'One More Angel in Heaven', 'Potipah', 'Song of the King', 'Those Canaan Days' and 'Benjamin Calypso'.

Jacob & Sons

This song uses only three chords: I, IV and ♭VII – the major triad based on **flattened seventh** note of the major scale, which acts as a substitute for the dominant (V). A major scale with a flattened seventh is known as the **Mixolydian mode** and is widely used in rock and folk music. The verse uses a simple repeated four-bar chord sequence, whereas the chorus uses a repeated two-bar chord sequence. Fill in both chord sequences for the original key of D major:

VERSE				
I	♭VII	IV	♭VII	I

CHORUS		
♭VII	IV	I

Any Dream Will Do

This song uses four major triads: I, II, IV and V, in a 32-bar song structure with a middle eight (rather than a verse and chorus form). Note: II is a *major* triad and Ic is the tonic chord with the dominant in the bass. Complete the table in the original key of C major:

Intro	I	IV	I	V					
Verse	I	V	I	IV	I	V	I	V	
Middle eight	IV	IV	II	II	Ic	V	V	V	
Ending	IV	I	IV	I	IV	I	IV	IV	I

Joseph: Spot the pastiche

Listen to five songs in styles which influenced numbers in *Joseph* and complete the table below. For the musical features common to both songs, you should particularly focus on tonality, rhythm and instrumentation. The first one is done for you.

Performer/Song/Link	Song in *Joseph* and musical style	Musical features in common
Edith Piaf 'Sous le Ciel de Paris' https://youtu.be/rlaVOvK8rYs	'Those Canaan Days' French *chanson*	Minor tonality Triple metre Accordion
Elvis Presley 'All Shook Up' https://youtu.be/_5v74TsY0R8		
Charlie McCoy 'Today I Started Loving You Again' https://youtu.be/ex_KtZqSkd8		
The Trinidad Steel-Band 'Liza' https://youtu.be/FiyPOxDfG5M?t=3m39s		
The Savoy Orpheans 'Could I? I Certainly Could' https://youtu.be/9Ix370p88oA		

Stephen Schwartz: 'Defying Gravity' from *Wicked*

Structure, Tonality, Tempo

Listen to the song with the score and complete the table below.

STRUCTURE		TONALITY		TEMPO
Section	**Bar**			
Intro 1	1	Chromatic		Colla voce
Dialogue 1	20	B major	F major	Andante
Verse 1				
Chorus 1				
Link 1				
Verse 2				
Chorus 2				
Dialogue 2				
Bridge 1				
Chorus 3				
Link 2				
Intro 2				
Bridge 2				
Chorus 4				
Link 3				
Coda				

Texture

- The introduction combines .... chords in the orchestra and .... vocal lines.

- The main texture in the song is

  ....

- In the choruses, the accompaniment is a more .... texture.

Dynamics & Articulation

- The dynamic markings in the song range from .... to ....

- There are several ....s and ....s (for

  example, in bars 22-23), particularly in the transitions from one section to the next

- The articulation marks include:

sf   ....

\>   ....

.   ...

⌣   ....

Rhythm & Metre

- Most of the song uses the time signature .... , but .... , ... and .... are also used.

- The melody uses .... (off-beat) rhythms

- The verses are accompanied by .... (off-beat) chords

- The choruses are accompanied by continuous ....

- The 2nd Dialogue and 1st bridge (bars 88-98) are accompanied by

  ....

Instrumentation

Write down the instruments in the correct families.

Woodwind	Brass	Percussion	Plucked strings	Bowed strings	Electronic

Melody

- The verses use perfect ……………………….. and ………………………… intervals.

- The 1st Bridge section uses the 'Unlimited' theme (in bars 93-94) – a seven-note melodic motif based on the song …………………………………………………………… (from the musical ……………………………….) but with a different …………………………… .

- Complete the notation of the 'Unlimited' theme below:

- The motif is repeated in bars 95-96 with the following change: ……

Harmony

- The song uses a variety of cadences, including a(n) ……………………….. cadence in bars 50-51 and a(n) ……………………….. cadence in bars 62-63.

- Most of the chords are major or minor ………………………. (three-note chords).

- Sometimes the chords have a ……………………… 2nd or 4th (e.g. in bar 21).

- ……………………… chords, where the fifth is sharpened, are found in bars 7 and 122.

- A ……………………………………… chord is used in bar 19.

The major scale and its triads

MAJOR SCALES use this pattern of tones (T) and semitones (S): TTSTTTS

C major

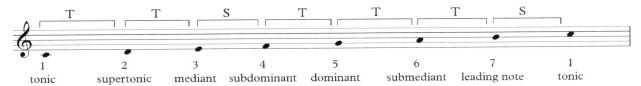

By keeping the same pattern of tones and semitones, a major scale can be built starting on any note (the resulting flats and sharps create the key signature):

G major

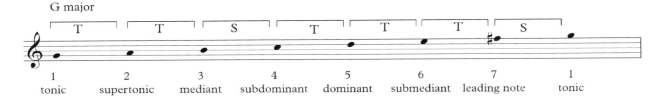

By adding a third and a fifth above each degree of the scale, you can form TRIADS (three-note chords). These can be labelled with Roman numerals. In major keys, three triads are MAJOR (use a capital Roman numeral), three are MINOR (lower case), and one is DIMINISHED (lower case with a degree symbol):

C major

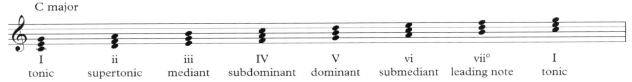

Exercises

Notate the following ASCENDING scales with flats or sharps (but no key signature). Watch the clefs!

1. E♭ major

2. F major

3. E major

Chords and Melody

Cadences

Strong chord progressions

Melody writing guidelines

1. Create a smooth wavy shape for each phrase (imagine 'joining the dots' of the melody)

2. Start each line on a chord note and then move up or down the scale

3. Only change direction in your scale-based melody (up or down) on a note in the underlying chord

4. Leap only occasionally, and always between notes which are both in the underlying chord

5. Use longer notes for the cadence at the end of each four-bar phrase

Composing Project 1: Songwriting

Brief

Compose a song using chosen lyrics. The song can be in any style (e.g. pop, rock, folk, classical etc.), and should have at least two distinct sections (e.g. verse and chorus). The melody should be singable and be based on a strong chord sequence.

Step 1 – Find your lyrics

See the different sets of lyrics to suit different moods and styles on the next page. Alternatively, you can choose or write your own lyrics, but you are strongly advised to check these with your teacher. You will not receive any credit for the lyrics themselves for GCSE music coursework, but you will receive credit for the way you set them to music. From now on, the 'verses' of the lyrics are referred to as 'stanzas', to avoid confusion with the 'verses' in your song.

Step 2 – Structure your song

Here are five of the most common musical forms used in songwriting:-

1. **Strophic** – this is where each stanza of text is set to the same music. If you choose this, try to create some variety within and between the verses.
2. **Binary** – first section one mood, second section contrasting mood. This might suit two verses of lyrics where, for example, the first section is sad but the second section is happy.
3. **Ternary** – first section one mood, second section different mood, then return to first section
4. **Verse and chorus** – where verse and chorus alternate: verse, chorus, verse, chorus etc.
5. **Pop song form** – Introduction, Verse 1, Chorus, Verse 2, Chorus, Middle 8, Chorus, Coda. This is the most complex of these structures, suiting lyrics in at least four stanzas, so you can have two verses, a chorus and a middle 8.

Most songs would normally have an introduction and usually a coda as well. Don't worry too much about these short sections at this stage – the music will probably come from your other material anyway.

Choose your musical form and label each stanza of your lyrics accordingly.

Step 3 – Set out the lyrics

For each section of the song, use a blank songwriting grid on the next page to write out the lyrics so they fit into four phrases, each phrase four bars long. Make sure there is a stressed syllable in the text at the beginning of each bar. At this stage the rhythm of the lyrics will probably suggest the time signature – usually two, three or four beats in a bar.

Some Lyrics for Songwriting

Ye Spotted Snakes

Ye spotted snakes with double tongue,
 Thorny hedgehogs, be not seen;
 Newts and blindworms, do no wrong,
 Come not near our fairy Queen.

Philomele, with melody
 Sing in our sweet lullaby;
 Lulla, lulla, lullaby, lulla, lulla, lullaby:
 Never harm
 Nor spell nor charm,
 Come our lovely lady nigh;
 So, good night, with lullaby.

Weaving spiders, come not here;
 Hence, you long-legged spinners, hence!
 Beetles black, approach not near;
 Worm nor snail, do no offence.

Philomele, with melody
 Sing in our sweet lullaby;
 Lulla, lulla, lullaby, lulla, lulla, lullaby:
 Never harm
 Nor spell nor charm,
 Come our lovely lady nigh;
 So, good night, with lullaby.

William Shakespeare

How Do I Love Thee?

How do I love thee? Let me count the ways.
I love thee to the depth and breadth and height
My soul can reach, when feeling out of sight
For the ends of being and ideal grace.
I love thee to the level of every day's
Most quiet need, by sun and candle-light.
I love thee freely, as men strive for right.
I love thee purely, as they turn from praise.
I love thee with the passion put to use
In my old griefs, and with my childhood's faith.
I love thee with a love I seemed to lose
With my lost saints. I love thee with the breath,
Smiles, tears, of all my life; and, if God choose,
I shall but love thee better after death.

Elizabeth Barrett Browning

Blow ye Winds Westerly

Come all you bold fishermen, listen to me,
I'll sing you a song of the fish in the sea.
So blow ye winds westerly, westerly blow,
We're bound to the southward, so steady we go.

Up jumps the fisherman, stalwart and grim,
And with his big net he scoops them all in.
So blow ye winds westerly, westerly blow,
We're bound to the southward, so steady we go.

First comes the bluefish a-wagging his tail,
He comes up on deck and yells, 'All hands make sail!'
So blow ye winds westerly, westerly blow,
We're bound to the southward, so steady we go.

Next come the herrings with their little tails,
They manned sheets and halyards and set all the sails.
So blow ye winds westerly, westerly blow,
 We're bound to the southward, so steady we go.

Next comes the porpoise with his short snout,
He jumps on the bridge and yells 'Ready about!'
So blow ye winds westerly, westerly blow,
We're bound to the southward, so steady we go.

Traditional

After Death

The curtains were half drawn, the floor was swept
And strewn with rushes, rosemary and may
Lay thick upon the bed on which I lay,
Where through the lattice ivy-shadows crept.
He leaned above me, thinking that I slept
And could not hear him; but I heard him say,
'Poor child, poor child': and as he turned away
Came a deep silence, and I knew he wept.
He did not touch the shroud, or raise the fold
That hid my face, or take my hand in his,
Or ruffle the smooth pillows for my head:
He did not love me living; but once dead
He pitied me; and very sweet it is
To know he still is warm though I am cold.

Christina Rossetti

Step 4 - Write chord sequence

Now choose a key (C major if you're not sure) and work out a strong chord sequence to go with the lyrics in each section. Make sure each phrase ends with a cadence and that the chord progressions work well – there are further ideas on the songwriting grid. Typically there would be one chord per bar, although in places you may want to have two chords per bar and in other places you might want to repeat a chord in a subsequent bar.

Start and end your section with the tonic chord (I) and see page 20 for cadences and strong chord progressions.

Which section of the song?_____

1st phrase	Chords				
	Lyrics				
2nd phrase	Chords				
	Lyrics				
3rd phrase	Chords				
	Lyrics				
4th phrase	Chords				
	Lyrics				

Which section of the song?_____

1st phrase	Chords				
	Lyrics				
2nd phrase	Chords				
	Lyrics				
3rd phrase	Chords				
	Lyrics				
4th phrase	Chords				
	Lyrics				

Step 5 – Choose whether to sing or notate the melody

The chord sequence you have composed forms the foundation for the all-important melody (tune) of your song. You have two choices when composing the melody: you can either **sing it** or **notate it** on software such as A computer notation program. Choose carefully, because there are pros and cons for both. When you have chosen, complete the relevant steps below.

	Pros	Cons	Steps
Singing the melody	• Much quicker to compose • More likely to be natural and song-like	• You might feel embarrassed about performing and/or recording your own voice	6, 10
Notating the melody (on computer software)	• The computer will play exactly what you have notated • You can work out which notes to use in the melody to fit the chords	• Can take much longer • Some rhythms might be hard to notate accurately, particularly syncopated rhythms in popular styles	7, 8, 9, 10

Step 6 – Work out your melody (singing method)

Play the chord sequence for each four-bar phrase over and over again on the piano/keyboard. When you are confident with playing the chord sequence for the first four-bar phrase, start chanting (speaking rhythmically) the lyrics over the top of the chords. Then start singing any pitches that sound natural with the chord sequence. When you have worked out the first phrase, make sure you remember and/or record it straight away.

Step 7 – Notate your chord sequence

From the Quick Start menu on Software such as A computer notation program, type in 'Voice and keyboard' to set up your score with the time signature (and the key signature, if you are not in C major/A minor). Notate the chords in note lengths that take up the whole duration of each chord, with the triad (three-note chord) in the right hand and the bass note (which is the first note of the chord, an octave lower) in the left hand. Then press **ctrl+K** to notate the chord symbol above each bar, e.g.:

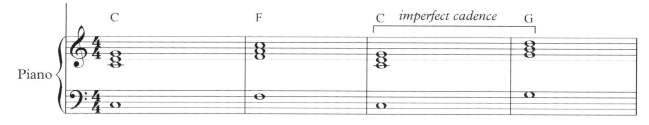

Step 8 – Notate the rhythm of the melody

You have already divided up the text into bars on your songwriting grid. Now use the natural rhythms of the text to notate the note lengths for the first phrase (just use the first note of each chord as the pitch for now). Make sure that the **emphasised** syllables of the text fall on the **strongest** beats in the music. Then use **ctrl+L** to type in the lyrics under the rhythm, separating the syllables with a dash (-):

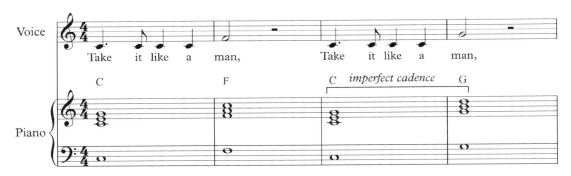

Step 9 – Notate the pitches of your melody

Now change some of the pitches of the melody to give it some shape. Try to make each four-bar phrase into a recognisable **melodic contour** (the shape you get if you 'join the dots'). Here are some common melodic contours:

- Start and end each phrase on a **chord note** (i.e. a note that is in the underlying chord).
- Use your melodic contour to guide you going up and down the scale of your chosen key (e.g. C major)
- The **range** of the melody should be between an octave and an octave and a half.
- Most of the notes in the melody should be **stepwise** (i.e. next-door neighbours in the scale) or the same as the previous note.
- You can **leap** occasionally from one chord note to the next chord note, for example between C and E if the chord is C major.

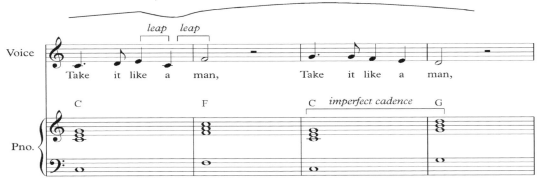

Step 10 – Structure phrases within your sections

Now you have composed your first phrase, you should repeat the melody-writing process for the other phrases in the section of the song you are working on (e.g. verse or chorus). You should repeat at least some bits of melody and/or rhythm you have already used. This is essential to make your melody 'hold together'; otherwise it will sound disjointed. This could be as simple as copying a melody which is the same apart from the cadence:

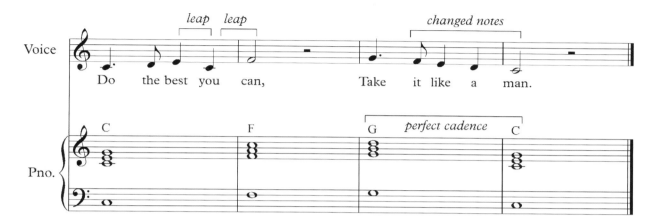

A History of Film Music

The earliest film music was played live by a pianist or organist in the pit of the theatre. The player would watch the screen and <u>improvise</u> accordingly. In larger cinemas, orchestras played mostly popular classics. In 1908 the Romantic French composer Saint-Saëns wrote the first original score, for a film called *The Assassination of the Duc de Guise*.

As film genres became established, so too did film music fall into genres within specially composed collections. These were classified under various headings for 'stock' scenes: fire, confusion, storm, stealth, romance, and so on. Conductors would go through the film and choose appropriate pieces. Players were then given cues during the film, for example, 'Chase No. 1 (Book 6)', or 'Love Theme No.3 (Book 2).

The invention of Vitaphone in 1926 allowed a <u>'soundtrack'</u> to be recorded alongside the picture frames on the celluloid. Although stock recordings were used at first, the musical possibilities of the soundtrack attracted many composers. Dramatic, tightly <u>synchronized</u> scores were written for films such as *King Kong* (Max Steiner, 1931) and *Captain Blood* (Erich Korngold, 1935). Symphonic scores by 'classical' composers, also heard in the concert hall, included *Henry V* (William Walton, 1944) and *Scott of the Antarctic* (Ralph Vaughan Williams, 1948).

After the war, film music was drawn from a wider range of styles, including light music, dance music, and jazz. Popular film musicals, such as Bernstein's *West Side Story* (1961), with its catchy Latin and jazz influences, required the soundtrack to be recorded before the film. The growth in creativity demanded <u>sound editing</u>, so music could be literally tailored to fit a scene.

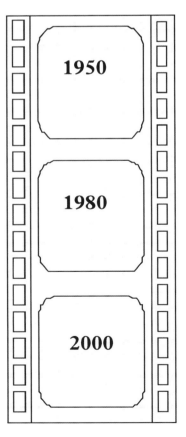

At the end of the 1970s, the modern <u>blockbuster</u> was born. These are hugely expensive but highly commercial films with big stars and special effects. Directors such as Steven Spielberg and George Lucas worked with the composer John Williams to create brilliant orchestral scores for *Jaws* (1975), *Star Wars* (1977), and *Close Encounters of the Third Kind* (1981). Often, the unusual setting of such films inspires the composer to create a new sound, for example to describe space.

Many of today's film composers have turned to <u>electronic music</u>, reflecting the current trend for 'special effects' films. There are many parallels between the media of special visual effects and electronic music, not least because both are usually produced on a computer. There are also now some women in the traditionally male-dominated world of film composers. One of these is Anne Dudley, who mixed her own incidental music (influenced by a pop background) with 'seventies dance hits in *The Full Monty* (1997).

A History of Film Music: Questions

1. Explain the following terms, underlined in the text:-

improvise
soundtrack
synchronized
sound editing
blockbuster
electronic music

2. What invention, in which year, effectively ended live music in the cinema?

3. What are the limitations of 'stock' film music?

4. For each of the following films, give the date, name the composer, and briefly describe the style of the music:

King Kong
West Side Story
The Full Monty
Star Wars
Henry V
The Assassination of the Duc de Guise

5. What is different about the way soundtracks are recorded for film musicals? Why?

TOTAL [20]

John Williams: *Star Wars* Theme

Listen to the whole piece, with or without the score, and answer the questions below.

Melody

How would you describe the melody of the opening section? ....

Harmony

Is the key major or minor? ....

Are the chords in the piece triads (three note chords) or something else? ....

Instrumentation

What are all these instruments collectively known as? ....

Which family of instruments is most prominent in the opening section? ....

Can you name any specific instruments? ....

Structure

Does the piece have an introduction? ....

Are any sections repeated? ....

What is the order of sections in the piece? ....

Rhythm

Are there any distinctive/repeated rhythms? ....

Can you notate or describe them? ....

Apart from film music, what style/original purpose does this music suggest? ....

Texture

Is the tune unaccompanied, accompanied, or combined with other tunes? ....

What word ending in –phonic best describes this texture? ....

Tempo

What is the starting tempo (speed) of the music? ....

Does the tempo change during the piece? ....

Listening Exercise on *Star Wars* Theme

Listen to the whole piece THREE times and answer the questions below.

1. Describe TWO musical ways in which the opening fanfare grabs the listener's attention. ....[2]

2. Which instruments play the first part (Section A) of the 'Main Title'? ....[1]

3. Which instruments play the middle section (Section B) of the 'Main Title'? Describe the articulation of this section. ....[2]

4. At the end of the 'Main Title', what effect is played by the harp? ....[1]

5. What repeated rhythm is played by the strings in the link section? What is the articulation? ... .[2]

6. In the 'Rebel Blockade Runner' section, what solo instrument briefly plays the melody? What are the dynamics of this section? ....[2]

7. What happens to the pitch of the strings in the link section after the 'Rebel Blockade Runner' section? ....[1]

8. Describe the timpani part in the March section. ....[2]

9. How does the tempo of the final section compare to the rest of the piece? ....[1]

10. Do you like or dislike this piece? Give a musical reason why. ....[1]

TOTAL [15]

Music for Stage and Screen: Comparison Exercise

Film version: 'Juliet'
from Franco Zeffirelli's *Romeo and Juliet* (1968)

1. What instrument starts the piece? ....
2. What instrument plays the tune for the second half of the first section? ....
3. How does the tempo of the middle section compare with the beginning of the piece? ....
4. What musical form does this piece use? ....

Musical version: 'I Feel Pretty'
from Leonard Bernstein's *West Side Story* (1957)

In *West Side Story*, Maria is the sister of the gangleader of the Sharks, Bernardo.

5. Describe the tempo of the piece...
6. How many beats in a bar are there? ....
7. What percussion instrument accompanied both the film and the musical version?...................
8. What kind of key does the piece begin and end in?...

Ballet version: 'Juliet, the young girl'
from Sergei Prokofiev's *Romeo and Juliet* (1935)

9. What instrument plays the tune at the beginning of the piece?.....................................
10. What instrument plays the tune when Count Paris is introduced? ....
11. What instrument plays the tune when Paris dances with Juliet? ....
12. How does the tempo of this section compare to the beginning of the piece? ....

Further discussion
What do all three pieces tell us about the character of Juliet? ....
....
....
....
....

Vocal Music

Listening to Early Vocal Music

Medieval Plainchant

O rubor sanguinis (Hildergard of Bingen, c.1150)

https://www.youtube.com/watch?v=WDeR9MeGNPg

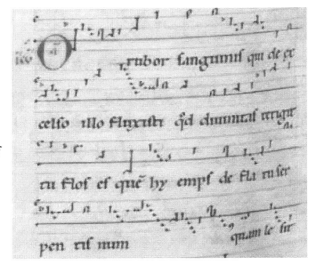

1. Which word best describes the tempo?
   a. Strict
   b. Free

2. Which words best describe the melody?
   a. Mostly disjunct
   b. Mostly conjunct
   c. Roughly half disjunct and half conjunct

3. Which word best describes the texture?
   a. Monophonic
   b. Polyphonic
   c. Heterophonic
   d. Homophonic

Medieval Troubadour song

A chanter m'er (Countess of Dia, c.1175)

https://www.youtube.com/watch?v=4NACeUqS2D4 (0.00-2.00)

1. What family does the instrument at the beginning belong to?
   a. Strings
   b. Woodwind
   c. Brass
   d. Percussion

2. Which words best describe the melody?
   a. Mostly disjunct
   b. Mostly conjunct
   c. Roughly half disjunct and half conjunct

3. What family does the instrument at the end belong to?
   a. Strings
   b. Woodwind
   c. Brass
   d. Percussion

Renaissance Motet

Ave Maria (Josquin Despres, c.1485)

https://www.youtube.com/watch?v=kxLv2pPiQVI (0.00-2.00)

1. Which 'phonic' word best describes the texture?
2. What other word describes the texture of the voices at the beginning?
3. How many different voice parts are there?
4. What are the names of these voice parts?

Baroque Oratorio

'And the glory of the Lord' from *Messiah* (Georg Frederic Handel, 1741)

https://www.youtube.com/watch?v=4egNeuAf0Bg

Time	Section	What can you hear?
0:00	Introduction	Texture Instruments Tempo Time signature
0:12	First vocal entries	Is the soprano/ contralto/tenor/bass singing the first tune? Which voices follow (in the right order!) And what do they sing?
0:19	New tune	Which voice introduces this tune?
0:41	?	What can you hear here?
0:46	3rd tune and 4th tune	Which voices sing these tunes first?
1:02		Can you describe any features of this section? What does the orchestra do while the choir are singing?

Researching Early Vocal Music

1. What were medieval wandering singers called?...[1]

2. In which country did Renaissance vocal particularly flourish?.......................................[1]

3. What vocal/theatrical art form was invented in about 1600, at the very beginning of the Baroque era? ....[1]

4. Define the following: [4]

   a. Oratorio...

   ....

   b. Cantata...

   ....

5. Name three Baroque composers and write the name of a large-scale vocal work written by each of them. [6]

Composer	Vocal work

6. What was the name of the puritan who ruled Britain between Charles I and Charles II and restricted music-making? ....[1]

7. What did Charles II introduce to accompany verse anthems? ....[1]

8. What is a masque? ....

....[2]

9. What is the name of Purcell's most famous opera which was performed at a girls' school in London in 1689? ....[1]

10. Public concerts became popular in the Baroque era. Europe's first purpose-built concert hall opened its doors in 1728 in Oxford. What was its name? ....[1]

11. Which of Handel's oratorios received its world première in Oxford on 10 July 1733?

....[1]

TOTAL MARKS [20]

Purcell: Music for a While

General

This piece is from the …………………………………….. era.

It was composed in the year …………..

It was part of the ………………………………. music for the play ……………………………. by ……………………………..

In the story, ………………………….. and two priests are trying to raise King …………………….. from the dead.

They refer to ………………………….., one of the Furies of ancient mythology, who has snakes for hair.

Instrumentation

………………………………..

………………………………..

………………………………..

………………………………..

Tempo and Dynamics

Are there tempo and dynamic markings in the score?…………………..

Structure

The ABA[1] structure (where A1 is shorter than A) is called .... form

Section	Rhythm	Melody	Texture	Harmony
Introduction (bars 1-3)				
Section A (bars 4-21) ('Music for a While...')				
Section B (bars 22-28) ('Till the snakes drop...')				
Section A[1] (bars 29-38) ('Music for a While...')				

Listening Exercise on 'Music for a While'

1. Which period of music history was this piece composed in? ....[1]

2. What technique is used in the bass line?..

   ....[1]

3. What two instruments make up the continuo accompaniment? ....

   ....[2]

4. What voice type is singing the melody? ....[1]

5. How does Purcell use word-painting on the word 'eternal'? ....[1]

6. Do you like or dislike this song? Give a musical reason why. ....

   ....[2]

TOTAL = 8 marks

Performing 'Music for a While'

Below is the three-bar ground bass (repeating bass pattern) used for most of the song, together with modern chord symbols. The full original sheet music is printed over the next three pages.

(N.B. The recorded version offered by Edexcel is at Baroque pitch, i.e. down a semitone)

Music for a while

from Orpheus Britannicus

Henry Purcell

The minor scale and its triads

NATURAL MINOR

A minor

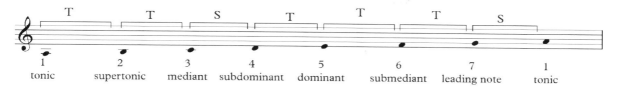

T	T	S	T	T	T	S

1 — tonic   2 — supertonic   3 — mediant   4 — subdominant   5 — dominant   6 — submediant   7 — leading note   1 — tonic

MELODIC MINOR

A minor

HARMONIC MINOR

A minor

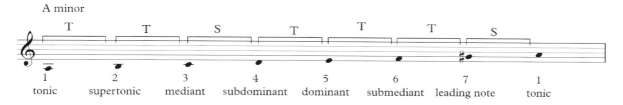

T	T	S	T	T	T	S

1 — tonic   2 — supertonic   3 — mediant   4 — subdominant   5 — dominant   6 — submediant   7 — leading note   1 — tonic

TRIADS

C major

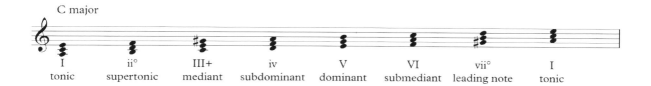

I — tonic   ii° — supertonic   III+ — mediant   iv — subdominant   V — dominant   VI — submediant   vii° — leading note   I — tonic

Composing Project 2: Ground Bass

What is a ground bass?

A ground bass is a short bass line, usually 4 or 8 bars long, that repeats throughout a piece, as the upper part(s) change. A ground bass is not an isolated line but really the foundation of a chord sequence.

Ground bass using root position triads

Here is an extract from one of the most famous ground basses, Pachelbel's *Canon* (transposed into C major), with the chords written above the bass line:

Descending bass line with first inversion triads

If you want more of a challenge, try a descending bass line, sometimes called a 'Lament' bass. This is ground bass that descends one step at a time, until the imperfect cadence at the end. Just writing a bunch of triads that go down a second is a very weak chord progression, so you have to use **first inversion** triads, which also provide variety. These are triads with the middle note in the bass. For example (note the imperfect cadence):

C	G/B	F/A	G	F	C/E	Dm	G

Chromatically descending bass line with first inversion triads

Even more of a challenge is a ground bass which descends **chromatically**. To achieve this, you have to 'borrow' chords from related keys; in other words, the music briefly passes through other keys (which will, of course, affect your melody later on). A chromatic ground bass works best in minor keys. Here is a famous example, 'When I am laid in earth' from Purcell's opera *Dido and Aeneas* (note the imperfect cadence):

Gm	D/F#	Dm/F	C/E	Cm/Eb	D	Bb	Cm	D

Step 1 – Choosing your instruments

The following instruments will help to create an authentic Baroque sound:

- The easiest single instrument is the **harpsichord**, as you can write the melody and/or chords in the right hand and the ground bass in the left hand. You can also use the harpsichord as a **continuo** instrument to play the chord sequence throughout the piece, if you use other instruments.
- The violin family is the mainstay of Baroque instrumental music: the **violin** for high melodies, the **viola** for middle melodies or harmonies, and **'cello** (short for violoncello) for the ground bass. (Beware: the viola uses the C clef, which is neither treble nor bass clef and therefore quite confusing. You can avoid this by using two or three different violin parts, like Pachelbel does in his *Canon*.)
- If you want to use woodwind instruments for the melody, choose the **flute** and/or **oboe** (the clarinet was not invented until the Classical era). The **bassoon** can play the bass line, although woodwind-only ensembles were far less common than woodwind solos with strings.
- Avoid brass and percussion instruments, as they only tended to be used for grand ceremonial or celebratory music in the Baroque era in a relatively large orchestra.

Step 2 – Compose your ground bass

Take your time composing the bass line as you're going to be stuck with it for the whole piece!

- Choose a key signature and time signature (the simplest are C major and 4/4).
- Work out a four-bar pattern with two different chords in each bar. The chord should change on the first beat of the bar and the next strongest beat in the bar.
- Start the pattern with the tonic chord (chord I; C in C major).
- End the pattern with an **imperfect cadence** from either chord ii (Dm in C major) or chord IV (F in C major) to chord V (G major in C major).
- For the chords in between, use strong progressions (up or down a fourth or fifth, down a third, up a second). Avoid diminished chords (vii° in all keys and ii° in minor keys).
- Label each chord using ctrl+K. This will be a useful point of reference when you're composing the melody later on.

Write your chord sequence below. Then enter it into a computer notation program and repeat it several times.

Step 3 – Add the chords (optional)

Either at the beginning of the piece, or once the ground bass has been played once through, you may wish to compose the three-note chords above the bass line in the upper part(s), and repeat them throughout the piece. Unless you are writing the chords for the harpsichord, the three notes of each chord should be split between three different parts. It doesn't matter which order they are in – you might want to rearrange them so that the chords don't jump around too much. If you are planning to write several parts above the bass line, you may prefer to reveal the harmony one line at a time.

Step 4 – Compose one melody note for each bass note

Compose one note of melody for each note of your ground bass. Remember you're composing a melody, so you should be aiming for mainly stepwise (conjunct) movement – in other words, most of the notes should be next to each other. To start, pick a note from the first chord (preferably not the same as the bass note), then continue the process with the other chords, using notes near to each other to create a pleasing melodic shape for these four bars. Here's how Pachelbel does it:

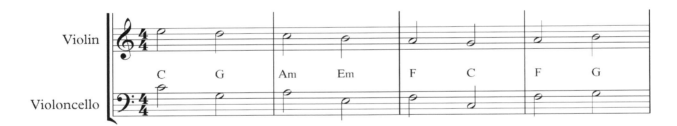

Step 5 – Compose another melody note for each note (optional)

Compose another four bars of melody also using one note per note of the ground bass, but use different notes from Step 3. Look at Pachelbel's middle line below:

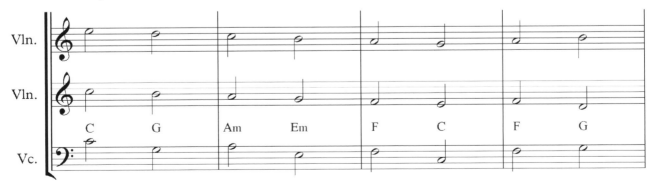

More advanced: composing a canon

If you're writing for two or more melodic instruments and want to create a **polyphonic** texture (rather than just using the other instruments to create homophonic chords), consider composing a **canon**, like Pachelbel does. To do this, copy and paste bars 5-8 of the first melodic instrument into bars 9-12 of the next melodic instrument (see Pachelbel's example above).

Step 6 – Compose two melody notes for each bass note

Compose another 4 or 8 bars of melody, this time with two melody notes for each bass note. For this to work properly:

- both notes should be in the underlying chord OR
- ONE note can be a **passing-note** – in other words, a note that fills the gap between two chord notes

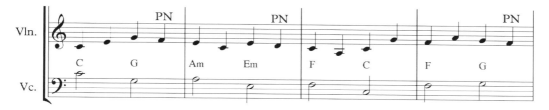

Step 7 – More rhythmic variety (optional)

Try other combinations of note-lengths for each bass note, like the dotted rhythm below:

More advanced: auxiliary notes

You can also see in the example above another type of non-chord note called an **auxiliary note**. This goes a step up or down from a chord note and then immediately back to the same chord note.

Step 8 – Suspensions (More advanced/optional)

Compose a version of 'one melody note per bass note' (see Step 4) with **suspensions**. For a suspension to work, you need to find two melody notes, each one above a different bass note, where the second note is both one step below the first and also a note that is NOT in the second chord. You can then either repeat or continue the first note when the bass note changes, creating a temporary harmonic tension which is resolved by going down to the chord note. Look how Pachelbel uses suspensions towards the end of his Canon to create and then dissipate the tension:

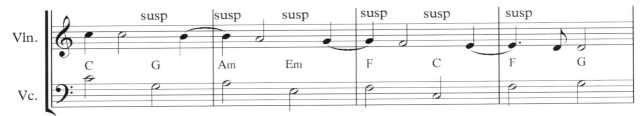

More advanced: double non-chord notes

If you are composing a canon (or other polyphonic texture), any double non chords (passing-notes, auxiliary notes or suspensions) must be separated by an interval of a **3rd** or a **6th**.

Step 9 – Structuring your piece as a whole

When you have composed all the four-bar sections you want to for a 1-2 minute piece, you should arrange them in an order which works best for the effect you want to create. Pachelbel uses an 'arc' structure, where the texture and rhythmic complexity increases towards the middle, and then becomes simpler again towards the end. (By definition, a ground bass is repeated, so it's hard to compose a completely different section of music; accordingly, musical structures such as binary or ternary form are not possible.)

The ending

Because your ground bass chord sequence ends with an imperfect cadence, which sounds inconclusive, you need to put one bar at the end which just contains the tonic chord (C in C major).

Step 10 – Finishing touches

- Title (right click on score, then Text > Title)
- Composer (right click on score, then Text > Composer)
- Date (right click on score, then Text > Lyricist)
- Tempo (right click on score, then Text > Tempo)
- Terraced dynamics (ctrl+E, then right-click for dynamic markings from *pp* to *ff*)
- Phrasing (select notes in a phrase, then press S)

Rock 'n' Roll

The original name of Rock music is Rock 'n' Roll. This started in the mid-1950s when white American artists like Bill Haley and Elvis Presley recorded songs written or inspired by Rhythm 'n' Blues, the popular music of African Americans in the late 1940s and early 1950s. It combined the style of the traditional country blues (typically sung as a solo accompanied by acoustic guitar or piano), with the more urban rhythm section of drum kit and plucked double bass, with other instruments such as brass and electric guitars. All these styles (country blues, rhythm 'n' blues and early rock 'n' roll) relied heavily on the twelve-bar blues structure.

Listening to 'Shake, Rattle 'n' Roll'

Compare two versions of this 1954 song:

- Rhythm 'n' Blues - Big Joe Turner (https://www.youtube.com/watch?v=YhELpSeeipg)
- Rock 'n' Roll - Bill Haley and the Comets (https://www.youtube.com/watch?v=KuDoa3f1EYQ)

'Shake, Rattle 'n' Roll'	Rhythm 'n' Blues Big Joe Turner	Rock 'n' Roll Bill Haley and the Comets
Instrumentation		
Harmony (chord sequence)		
Structure		
Melody		
Lyrics		

Performing 'Shake, Rattle 'n' Roll'

Work out the 12-bar blues in the keys of both version of the song.

Big Joe Turner's key ....Bill Haley's key ....

I	I	I	I
IV	IV	I	I
V	IV	I	I

I	I	I	I
IV	IV	I	I
V	IV	I	I

Now play through the 12-bar blues on keyboards or guitars in both of the above keys. Try these common keys as well: G, D, E, A. (Work out chords I, IV and V in each key before you try it.)

Rock Music in the 1960s

Listening: Neil Sedaka – 'Happy Birthday Sweet Sixteen' (1961)

https://www.youtube.com/watch?v=y5CUfVm1Si8

INTRO	VERSE 1 & REFRAIN	VERSE 2	MIDDLE 8	VERSE 3 & REFRAIN	REPEAT OF VERSE 3 & REFRAIN	OUTRO
8 bars	16 bars	16 bars	16 bars	16 bars	16 bars	8 bars
Tra la la la la la	Tonight's the night I've waited for…	What happened to that funny face?	When you were only six, I was your big brother	So, if I should smile with sweet surprise	So, if I should smile with sweet surprise	Tra la la

1. Which instrument plays chords in this song?..

2. Which percussion instruments are playing in this song?...

3. What instrument is playing the bass line?...

4. What family of orchestral instruments are also playing in the song?......................................

5. Compare the melody of the first and second phrases of each verse. ....

6. What interval separates the lead and backing voices?...

7. What happens to the key in the repeat of verse 3? ....
   ....

8. What key does the song end in? ....

The Beatles

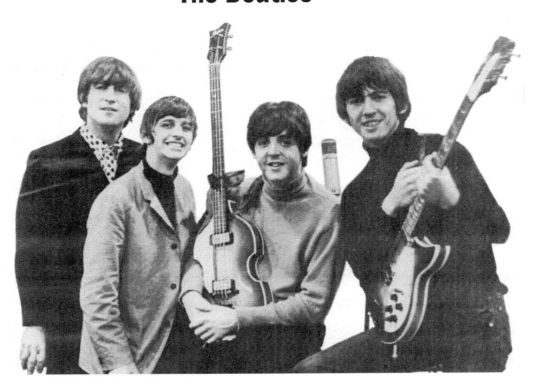

The Beatles – Paul McCartney, John Lennon, George Harrison and Ringo Starr – were a band from Liverpool which changed the face of rock 'n' roll, partly because of the original way in which they used harmonies and timbre in their songs.

Electric and Bass Guitars

Many rock 'n' roll bands used two electric guitars and a bass guitar (or electric bass). For example, in the Beatles, John Lennon played chords on the 'rhythm' guitar, George Harrison played solos and riffs (catchy repeating patterns) on the 'lead' guitar, and Paul McCartney played the bass line on the bass guitar.

Electric Guitar

At first glance, the bass guitar looks similar to an electric guitar – but there are some important differences. What are they?

Bass Guitar

(or Electric Bass)

Primary and Secondary Triads

Primary triads (chords I, IV and V; or C, F and G in C major) are the most important chords in any key. The triads based on the other four degrees of the scale are called **secondary triads**. In a major key, three of these secondary triads are minor chords and can be notated with lower case Roman numerals: ii, iii and vi. Secondary triads can be used for variety, often substituting for the major chord a third higher, particularly vi instead of I and ii instead of IV. (The one remaining triad, vii°, is based on the seventh degree of the scale, or leading note; this can be disregarded for the time being.)

For each of the minor chords Dm, Em and Am:

- Label the chord as a secondary triad in C major using a lower case Roman numeral
- Mark the three notes on the keyboard diagram
- Notate the three notes on the stave
- Write down the letter-names of the three notes

Chord of Dm   Chord of Em   Chord of Am

Notes in chord...............   *Notes in chord*...............   *Notes in chord*...............

If you complete the exercise above, repeat it below with a different major key of your choice.

Your chosen major key_____

Notes in chord...............   *Notes in chord*...............   *Notes in chord*...............

Rock Music in the 1970s

Rock Music in the 1970s became longer and more ambitious. Songs on **concept albums** were often linked thematically. The thicker textures were made possible by studio techniques such as **overdubbing**, a recording technique where the sounds are layered.

'Killer Queen' from *Sheer Heart Attack* (1974) by Queen

Structure

Here are the sections of the song in a jumbled order:

Instrumental	Verse 2	Chorus 3	Outro	Guitar solo	Verse 3	Verse 1	Chorus 2	Chorus 1

Rearrange these sections below. The first words of each section are given to help you.

She keeps a Moët and Chandon	She's a killer queen	[no words]	To avoid complications	She's a killer queen	[no words]	Drop of a hat	She's a killer queen	[no words]

Rhythm and Metre

This song is played in 12/8, with the occasional bar in 6/8. These are both **compound time signatures**, which divide each beat into 3 instead of 2 or 4 in a simple time signature. In a compound time signature, the upper number represents the number of subdivided beats, as opposed the main beats in a simple time signature. The lower number represents the note value of these subdivided beats – in this case, 8 means quavers.

There are lots of examples of **syncopation**, or offbeat rhythms, in the piece.

Instrumentation

Queen uses the typical instruments for a four-piece rock band (just like the Beatles). Find out what each of the members performed in the band:

Freddie Mercury .... Roger Taylor ....

Brian May .... John Deacon ....

Killer Queen – Analysis

Section	Melody	Harmony (chords)	Texture (incl. accompaniment)	Other musical features
Verse 1 'She keeps a Moët and Chandon' Bars 2-14				
Chorus 1 'She's a killer queen' Bars 15-22				
Instrumental Bars 23-26				
Verse 2 'To avoid complications' Bars 27-35				
Chorus 2 'She's a killer queen' Bars 36-43				
Guitar solo Bars 44-61				
Verse 3 'Drop of a hat' Bars 62-69				
Chorus 3 'She's a killer queen' Bars 70-78				
Outro Bars 79-end				

Listening to Vocal Music

Here are some words that are useful when describing vocal music.
Write the correct words next to their definitions.

Motif   Monophonic   Word-painting   Interval   Sequence   Voice type

Disjunct   Imitation   Homophonic   Melismatic   Conjunct   Syllabic

Vocal range   Consonance/   Ornamentation   Dissonance/   Portamento   Polyphonic
               concord   discord

	melody where the notes are mostly close together (stepwise/scalic)
	melody where the notes are mostly leaping (i.e. melodic intervals of a 3rd of greater)
	one note to each syllable of text
	several notes to each syllable of text
	(Italian for 'carrying') – sliding from one pitch to another
	distance from one note to the next: 2nd, 3rd, 4th, 5th, 6th, 7th, 8^{ve} (octave)
	interval from the lowest note to the highest note, e.g. an octave
	where the music reflects the meaning of the text (e.g. 'eased')
	notes which go well together (e.g. a 3rd)
	notes which clash together (e.g. a 2nd)
	extra notes added to decorate the melody
	soprano (high female), alto (low female), tenor (high male), bass (low male)
	one or more voices singing the same melody without accompaniment
	two or more melodies at the same time
	melody and accompaniment
	where one voice or instrument copies another
	the same melody shape and rhythm repeated higher or lower
	a distinctive fragment of melody, repeated and transformed in a piece

Fusions

Seventh chords

A seventh chord is a triad (three-note chord) with an extra note a seventh above the root.

This creates a chord with four notes:

Triad   Root + 7th   Triad + 7th

The stacking of thirds which makes a triad continues with the seventh chord, as the seventh is a third above the top note of the triad.

The following seventh chords can all be constructed from various major and minor scales. Play them on a keyboard and listen to the distinct sound of each one.

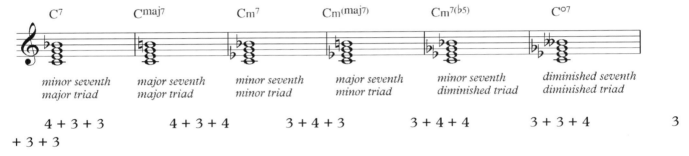

4 + 3 + 3   4 + 3 + 4   3 + 4 + 3   3 + 4 + 4   3 + 3 + 4   3 + 3 + 3

Most jazz harmony is based on seventh chords.

Samba em Prelúdio

Listen to the chords in the fourth stanza of 'Samba em Prelúdio' (beginning 'Es tou tão sozinha), following the score if possible.

Here is a simplified version of the chord sequence, using one chord per bar. Notate the given chord sequence on the staves provided

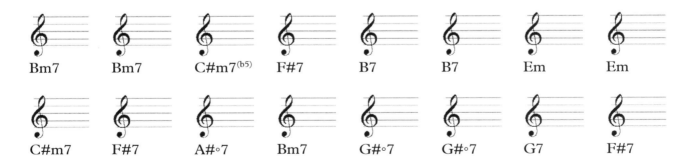

Now play the chord sequence on a keyboard, working out the notes one at a time.

If you get this far, try playing the chords in time with a bossa nova rhythm on the keyboard.

Composing Project 3: Blues

Compose a Blues piece for one or more instrument(s).

Step 1 – Choose your instruments

- The simplest single instrument to write for is the piano, because you can write your melody in the right hand (treble clef) and accompaniment in the left hand (bass clef).
- If you prefer, the accompaniment could be played by a single instrument that can play chords (typically piano or guitar) OR three or four medium-pitched instruments which share the notes of the chords.
- You may wish to add a pizzicato (plucked) double bass, or, for a more modern sound, the electric bass, to reinforce the bass line.
- High-pitched melodic instruments commonly found in jazz are the saxophone, trumpet or clarinet – but beware – these are all transposing instruments and therefore read music in different keys.
- You can also add a drum kit – an authentic swing rhythm would use brushes on the ride cymbal ('ten-to-ten'), punctuated by off-beat snare drum notes.

Step 2 – Compose your chord sequence

Work out your chord sequence on a piano, keyboard or guitar. A basic 12-bar blues sequence is as follows. The chord is written as a Roman numeral (I, IV or V); the chords in the key of C major are in brackets.

Bar 1 I (C)	Bar 2 I (C)	Bar 3 I (C)	Bar 4 I (C)
Bar 5 IV (F)	Bar 6 IV (F)	Bar 7 I (C)	Bar 8 I (C)
Bar 9 V (G)	Bar 10 IV (F)	Bar 11 I (C)	Bar 12 I (C)

Variants on the 12-bar blues (advanced)

Different keys

You can write your chord sequence in any key. As a general rule, string instruments prefer sharp keys and wind instruments prefer flats. E major is a particular favourite of guitarists. Remember if you are writing for transposing instruments (for example, clarinet in Bb, trumpet in Bb or alto saxophone in Eb), those instruments will be reading the music in a different key, so spare a thought for which key they will be reading in.

Seventh chords

Jazz and blues uses seventh chords as its basic building-block, rather than the triad (three-note chord). You can form a seventh by adding a minor seventh above the root to the triad, so, for example, C7 is C-E-G-Bb.

Chord substitutions

There are many variants on the chord sequence above, if you want to make your blues more harmonically adventurous. Try the following:

- Bar 2 – IV7 (F7 in C major)
- Bar 6 - #IVdim7 – diminished seventh chord on the sharpened fourth (F#-A-C-Eb in C major)
- Bar 8, 9, 10 – VI7-ii7-V7 (A7-Dm7-G7 in C major)
- Bar 12 – V7 (G7 in C major) – for when the chord sequence repeats, but not at the end of the piece

Step 3 – Starting your score in a computer notation program

Once you have worked out your chord sequence, start a new score in a computer notation program with your chosen instruments. Choose a 4/4 time signature and your chosen key signature. Above the first bar, right-click for the menu and go to Text>Tempo. Give a tempo marking (and preferably a metronome mark) which includes the word '**swing**', to make sure the piece is performed with 'swung' quavers (so the beats are divided into quavers lasting two-thirds of a beat and one-third of a beat, instead of two equal halves).

Step 4 – Choose an accompanying pattern

Listen to the 30 accompanying patterns on the next page and choose one appropriate for your style of blues. These are written for the left hand of the piano, but they can be transposed into the treble clef for guitar or split into three or four separate instrumental parts.

More advanced: 'comping' rhythms

You could write your own 'comping' pattern, for example with the piano playing syncopated chords above a walking bass, created from chord notes and passing-notes:

Step 5 – Compose a 2-bar motif

Compose a two-bar **syncopated** rhythmic motif using crotchets, quavers, dotted crotchets and triplets (create triplets by selecting a quaver and pressing ctrl+3 on the main computer keyboard, not the numeric keypad). You can achieve the syncopated effect by tying notes across the beats. Here are some one-bar examples, but there are many more:

Examples of syncopated swing rhythms

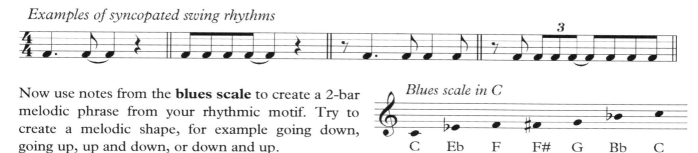

Now use notes from the **blues scale** to create a 2-bar melodic phrase from your rhythmic motif. Try to create a melodic shape, for example going down, going up, up and down, or down and up.

Blues scale in C

C   Eb   F   F#   G   Bb   C

Step 6 – Use call-and-response to create an 'answering' phrase

Now compose a 2-bar 'answering' phrase, again with a syncopated rhythm and pitches from the blues scale. The phrase should have both similarities to, and differences from the first phrase: for example, using the same rhythm, but going down instead of going up:

Example of two 2-bar phrases using call-and-response

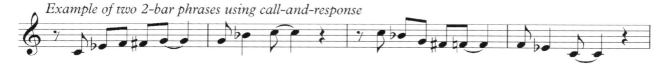

Step 7 – Develop the 4-bar phrase for the rest of the 12-bar blues

The simplest way to extend the 4-bar phrase you have written is simply to repeat it twice, so it becomes a repeated **riff** (*aaa* form). However, you may wish to create one or two contrasting 4-bar phrases by repeating Steps 5 and 6. A common way of structuring the melody in the blues is *aab* form, but you could also create *abc* (or through-composed) form.

Step 8 – Add some authentic blues touches (advanced)

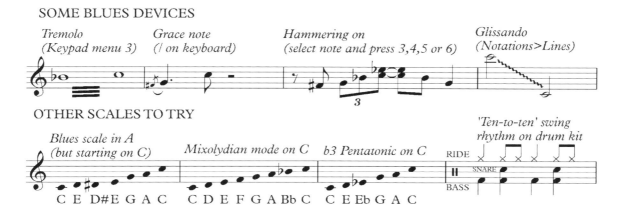

SOME BLUES DEVICES

Tremolo (Keypad menu 3)   Grace note (/ on keyboard)   Hammering on (select note and press 3,4,5 or 6)   Glissando (Notations>Lines)

OTHER SCALES TO TRY

Blues scale in A (but starting on C)   Mixolydian mode on C   b3 Pentatonic on C   'Ten-to-ten' swing rhythm on drum kit

C E D#E G A C   C D E F G A Bb C   C E Eb G A C

Step 9 - Extend your piece using variations

Jazz pieces usually take the form of a **Theme and Variations**, finishing with a repeat of the theme:

Theme ('Head') – One or more Variations ('Solos') - Theme ('Head')

For a 12-bar blues, each variation would be 12 bars long, following the same basic chord progression as the theme itself. Repeat Steps 4-8 to create each 12-bar variation with a different melody and accompanying pattern. If you are writing for more than one melodic instrument, you could assign a different variation (solo) to each instrument – like Miles Davis does in 'All Blues'.

The number of variations will depend on the tempo of your piece, how much you can compose in the 10-hour time limit for completing the controlled assessment, and the 1-2 minute running time of the piece itself.

Step 10 – Finishing touches

You have already supplied a tempo marking in Step 3. Now add dynamics and articulation markings such as accents, staccato, marcato and phrase marks. Don't forget to right-click above the first stave, select Text and to add the Title, Composer and Date (use the Lyricist position for the date).

Here are two standard endings for the blues, lasting two bars each:

Some Blues Accompanying Patterns

These are all based on the C chord - you can transpose them into other chords and keys

Swung quavers ♩=120

Patterns 27-30 last for TWO bars each

Esperanza Spalding: Samba em Prelúdio

Type of voice.............................. instruments .... and ....

Musical style............................. from .... language of lyrics ....

Bars	Section	Instrumentation/ Texture	Rhythm/ Tempo	Melody/ Harmony	Dynamics/ other
1-3	Intro				
4-21	Verse 1				
19-22	Break				
23-54	Verse 2				
55-87	Instrumental				
88-104	Verse 3				
105-end	Coda				

Glossary

Write definitions in your own words.

Mordent..

Syllabic..

Melismatic...

Rubato..

Monophonic...

Counterpoint/contrapuntal...

Clave (1)..................... .... (2)...

Seventh chord...

Extended chord..

Afro Celt Sound System: Release

Context

Fusion of ………………… music and …………………… music released in the year ……………

Voice/Instruments

Fill in the left-hand column of the Instruments/Texture table with the answer to each clue

Vocal sounds

1. African singer in the 'griot' tradition …………………………………………………………………
2. Sinéad O'Connor (Irish pop star) ………………………………………………………………………
3. Iarla Ó Lionáird (Irish folk singer) ……………………………………………………………………
4. Short recorded sound 'triggered' electronically ……………………………………………………

Western (European/American) pop instruments

5. Amplified high-pitched plucked string instrument with 6 strings ………………………………
6. Amplified low-pitched plucked string instrument with 4 strings …………………………………
7. Electronic keyboard instrument with a variety of sounds ………………………………………
8. (Two) electric keyboard instruments imitating the sound of another keyboard instrument where hammers hit the strings ……………………………………………………………………
9. Collection of percussion instruments including bass drum, snare drum and cymbals……………

European folk instruments

10. String instrument with medieval origins with a cranked-turned wheel rubbing against the strings ………………………………………………………………………………………………
11. Hand-held keyboard instrument powered by bellows……………………………………………
12. Folk name for the highest bowed string instrument………………………………………………
13. Shallow hand-held drum from Ireland played with a double-headed drumstick…………………
14. Shallow hand-held drum with jingles ………………………………………………………………
15. Irish bagpipes operated by bellows squeezed under the elbow …………………………………
16. Large tin whistle………………………………………………………………………………………

African instruments

17. Hourglass-shaped drum with the double heads tightened by cords running down the length of the drum which are tightened under the arm to create changes and slides in pitch ……………………
18. Harp with 21 strings, resonating in a half a large gourd, covered with skin …………………………

Accordion	*Electric guitar*	*Kora*	*Talking drum*
Bass guitar	*Electric pianos*	*Low whistle*	*Tambourine*
Bodhrán	*Female voice*	*Male voice (African)*	*Uillean pipes*
Breath sample	*Fiddle*	*Male voice (Irish)*	
Drum kit	*Hurdy Gurdy*	*Synthesiser*	

Afro Celt Sound System – Listening

This piece uses a **layered** texture, where several different parts or 'layers' are added and removed to create contrast. The unity in this, and many other layered pieces, is created by having each instrument playing a **'loop'** (or **ostinato**).

Instruments Write the instruments/voices in the left hand column of the table below (you can use the clues to help you)

Texture Complete the table below to show which layers are heard in which section of the piece. You can use the anthology and page 140 of the textbook to help you.

....	Intro			Verse 1				Verse 2			Solos				Verse 3			Build/outro				
Time	0:00	0:48	1:17	1:38	1:55	2:15	2:34	2:55	3:12	3:31	3:51	4:10	4:29	4:34	4:55	5:12	5:31	5:51	6:00	6:19	6:38	6:59
Vocal sounds																						
1.																						
2.																						
3.																						
4.																						
Western pop instruments																						
5.																						
6.																						
7.																						
8.																						
9.																						
European folk instruments																						
10.																						
11.																						
12.																						
13.																						
14.																						
15.																						
16.																						
African instruments																						
17.																						
18.																						

Exam Question practice on Afro Celt – Texture

The **layered** texture is an important feature of 'Release', as the gradual addition of different instruments and voices (mostly performing **ostinati** or **loops**) shapes the piece as a whole and creates much of the interest for the listener.

The listening examination might have a question like this:

Describe the texture during the first minute of the piece. [6]

....
....
....
....
....
....

How can you answer this question well to score full marks? The examiner is looking for six points.

First, you should summarise (in one word) the overall texture of the piece (clue: the word is printed above).

This piece uses a .... texture.

This particular type of texture involves different instruments/voices coming in one at a time, and that explains why you are going to describe those sounds for the rest of your answer.

Then, using short sentences, identify the instruments/voices in the order they come in, for example:

At the beginning, we hear the .... (clue: electronic sound)

Then, a .... starts to play. (clue: African drum)

Next, we hear a .... (clue: percussion, but not drum)

Then a .... voice is heard. (clue: gender, continent)

As the voice stops, a .... starts to play. (clue: Irish drum)

Afro Celt – other elements

Tonality and harmony

- Neither major nor minor, but _____
- Most of the piece uses notes from the _____ mode (mark the flats below):

    C   D   Eb   F   G   Ab   Bb   C

- The uilleann pipes solo uses notes from the _____ mode (mark the flats below):

    C   D   Eb   F   G   A   Bb   C

Rhythm, metre and tempo

- Time signature: _____
- _____ tempo at beginning
- _____ tempo begins halfway through introduction (100 beats per minute)
- Use of _____ (offbeat rhythms) and occasional _____ (three equal notes in one beat)
-

Melody

- Vocal melody mostly based around opening _____ (short, distinctive pattern)
- Solo parts play melodies based on _____ tunes (musical style)

4	*Dorian*	*modal*	*syncopation*
4	*folk*	*moderate*	*triplets*
Aeolian	*free*	*motif*	

Instrumental Music 1700-1820

Baroque Instruments

The Baroque Era (1600-1750) takes its name from the Portuguese word 'barocco', meaning a type of jewellery. Like the jewellery, Baroque music is highly decorated: sometimes with ornaments such as trills and often with counterpoint (more than one tune at the same time).

Below are twelve instruments commonly used in Baroque music. Can you name them?

Can you identify the solo instruments in the following pieces by J. S. Bach?

1. Toccata and Fugue https://www.youtube.com/watch?v=IVJD3dL4diY
2. Chaconne https://www.youtube.com/watch?v=myXOrVv-fNk
3. Chaconne (arranged) https://youtu.be/_ChKsMjIMFw
4. Prelude https://www.youtube.com/watch?v=PCicM6i59_I
5. Prelude (arranged) https://www.youtube.com/watch?v=cyDFhRk04dU

Now listen to the set work from the Baroque period (Johann Sebastian Bach: Brandenburg Concerto No. 5 in D major, 3rd movement) and note down the instruments you hear.

....

....

Bach's Brandenburg Concerto No. 5

- Bach's Brandenburg Concerto No. 5 is a _____ from the _____ era
- The solo instruments are _____, _____ and _____
- The third (last) movement is a mixture of _____ and _____ forms

Word list

Answer – the subject in a fugue, played a fourth/fifth higher or lower while the subject continues

Concerto grosso – a Baroque concerto for two or more soloists, usually in three movements (fast-slow-fast)

Concertino – the group of soloists in a concerto gross

Counterpoint/contrapuntal – polyphonic instrumental music

Countersubject – the second melody in a fugue, which fits with the subject

Dialogue – 'conversation' between two instruments or voices

Exposition (in a fugue) – first section where the different parts first play the subject/countersubject

Fugue – contrapuntal musical form with an exposition, middle section and coda

Ripieno (Italian for 'full') – the rest of the orchestra (usually only strings) in a concerto grosso

Stretto – where the entries of the subject overlap later in a fugue

Subject – the first, main melody in a fugue

Ternary – musical form with same outer sections (A) and a contrasting middle section (B): ABA

Trill – ornament using rapidly alternating notes next to each other

Triplet – three equal notes in the space of two

Bach - Analysis

Section	Musical features
A Bars 1-78	Bars 1-2 - _____ played by solo _____ in a _____ texture
	Bar 3 _____ played by solo _____ in a _____ texture, while the solo _____ plays the _____
	Bar 9 – solo _____ plays the _____ in the left hand
	Bar 11 – solo _____ plays the _____ in the right hand
	Bars 19 and 21 – solo _____ plays a _____ to sustain the notes
	Bars 39-41 – subject played in both hands of _____ in _____
	Bar 52 _____ between solo _____ and solo _____ using _____ rhythms
B Bars 79-232	
A Bars 233-310	see above – repeat of first A section (bars 1-78)

Bach's Brandenburg Concerto No. 5 – score

Wider Listening: The Four Seasons

Vivaldi: 'Winter' from the Four Seasons, first movement
Antonio Vivaldi (1678-1741)

Vivaldi was born in Venice, Italy, which is where he spent most of his life. His father, a professional musician at St Mark's Church, taught him to play the violin, and the two often performed together. Vivaldi became a Catholic priest and then Director of Music at the Pietà, a Venetian orphanage for young girls, a position he held for the rest of his life. The orchestra of this institution became famous, and people came from miles around the hear Vivaldi's talented students perform the music he had written for them. Vivaldi wrote operas, sonatas and choral works, but is particularly known for his **concertos** (he composed over 500, although many have been lost). A concerto is a piece, usually in three movements, for soloist(s) and orchestra. One of the most famous sets is *The Four Seasons*, which were composed with some poems describing the seasons.

The Four Seasons were written in about 1720, the same time as Bach's *Brandenburg* Concertos. Each of the concertos in *The Four Seasons*, has three movements in the pattern **fast-slow-fast**. They are all concertos for the **solo violin**. Vivaldi provided a sonnet (poem) with each concerto to indicate the 'story' the music was telling – *The Four Seasons* is therefore an early example of **programme music**.

Listen to the music with the score and complete the table below.

Bar	Section (Ritornello or Solo Episode)	Key	Other musical features	Text from poem
1				Shivering from the cold
12				Horrid wind
19				Running and stamping of feet
26				
39				
44				Teeth chattering
47				

The Classical Era (1750-1820)

1. **Grace and elegance** The Classical Era admired grace and elegance of melody and form, with evenly-balanced phrases.
2. **Clear textures** The textures were clear and uncluttered (example: Alberti bass). Polyphony was much less common.
3. **Strings at core of the orchestra** The strings remained at the heart of the classical orchestra. The violins were split into two and the double basses played the same as the 'cellos, creating a four-part texture.
4. **A woodwind section** In addition to the <u>flute, oboe, and bassoon</u> (the recorder was no longer used in the orchestra), the <u>clarinet</u> was invented in the Classical era. These four instruments almost always used in pairs as a section.
5. **Some brass and percussion instruments** The <u>trumpet, French horn, and timpani (kettle drums)</u> were used more often than the Baroque era. The <u>trombone</u>, although not a regular member of the orchestra until Beethoven's later symphonies, was used for church and other solemn music. The trumpet and horn were still 'natural', which meant they had a limited number of notes, and the timpani only had two notes.
6. **Sonata form** The most popular form for the first movement of sonatas, symphonies, string quartets, and concertos, was sonata form. The simplest way to understand this is to compare it to a three-act drama, where two characters (tunes in different keys) are introduced; there is some conflict between them, and then the two are heard in the same key.
7. **Symphony** The new large-scale form for orchestra, derived from the Baroque suite. The Classical symphony is usually in four movements: (1) sonata form (see above); (2) slow; (3) minuet and trio, and (4) finale. The sonata, concerto, and string quartet followed a similar plan, although the concerto tended to omit the minuet and trio.

Forms and Genres

- **SYMPHONY** see (7) above. This and the forms below followed more or less the same three- or four-movement plan.
- **SONATA** a piece in several movements for solo instrument and accompaniment. If the solo instrument was a piano, no further accompaniment was necessary.
- **CONCERTO** a piece for solo instrument and orchestra in several (usually three) movements.
- **STRING QUARTET** a piece for two violins, viola, and 'cello in several movements.
- **OPERA** a drama set to music and performed by solo singers, chorus, and orchestra. Arias were still common, although not always in ternary form. Recitative was sometimes accompanied by orchestra. Ensembles (numbers for several singers) were now used. 'Serious' operas were going out of fashion, and comic operas were popular.

Composers and Music

Franz Josef HAYDN (1732-1809) *Austria*
- 83 **String quartets** and 104 **Symphonies**

Wolfgang Amadeus MOZART (1756-1791) *Austria*
- **Operas**, e.g. *The Marriage of Figaro, Don Giovanni, The Magic Flute*
- **Concertos**, for piano, violin, and woodwind and 41 **Symphonies** inc. No.40 in G minor

Ludwig van BEETHOVEN (1770-1827) *Germany*
- 9 **Symphonies**, including No. 9 'Choral' ('Ode to Joy') and one **Opera**, *Fidelio*
- 16 **String Quartets** and **Concertos**, including 5 for piano and 1 for violin

Franz Peter SCHUBERT (1797-1828) *Austria*
- Over 600 **Songs**, including *The Trout, The Erl-King*; 9 **Symphonies**

Sonata Form

Sonata form, developed during the **Classical Era** (1750-1830), was used by composers for most first **movements** of **symphonies**, **string quartets**, **sonatas** and **concertos**. It is a large-scale structure for organising musical ideas. Looking at the overall picture, it is a type of **ternary form** (ABA):

A	B	A
EXPOSITION	DEVELOPMENT	RECAPITULATION

The **Exposition** is often repeated, resulting in AABA form (which is still a type of ternary form). The **Recapitulation** is labelled A because it is very similar, but not identical, to the Exposition.

Within each of these main sections, there are two musical ideas, known as the **first subject** and **second subject**, labelled 1 and 2 below:

A		B	A	
EXPOSITION		DEVELOPMENT	RECAPITULATION	
1	2	1 and/or 2	1	2

Within the Exposition and Recapitulation, the first and second subjects are played in that order (like binary form) and each one is in a fixed key. Within the Development, one or both of the subjects are mixed up, both in terms of keys and thematic material. Therefore, the first and second subjects go through several keys and keys are the most important factor in defining the structure:

A		B	A	
EXPOSITION		DEVELOPMENT	RECAPITULATION	
1	2	1 and/or 2	1	2
Home key	Related key	Other keys	Home key	Home key

There is also a **Bridge** passage modulating between the keys of the first and second subject in the Exposition. This is mirrored by a Bridge passage in the Recapitulation, which may briefly modulate, but ends up in the home key. The Exposition is finished off with a **codetta** ('little coda') and the Recapitulation (and the whole movement) is finished off with a **coda**:

A				B	A			
EXPOSITION				DEVELOPMENT	RECAPITULATION			
1	Bridge	2	Codetta	1 and/or 2	1	Bridge	2	Coda
Home key	Modulates	Related key	Related key	Other keys	Home key	Ends in home key	Home key	Home key

Label these sections on Clementi's Sonatina in C major on the next page.

SONATINA.

Op. 36, Nº 1.

Spiritoso.

M. CLEMENTI.

Composing Project 4: Piano Sonatina

*Compose a **sonatina** for **solo piano** in **sonata form**.*

Step 1 – Key scheme

Choose a home key to begin and end the piece. C major or A minor are the simplest keys, because there are no sharps or flats in the key signature, but you can to use another key signature if you wish. The 2nd subject of the Exposition should be a closely related key – usually the dominant or relative major/minor.

Write your chosen keys in the bottom row of this table. Leave the Development blank for now.

A EXPOSITION		B DEVELOPMENT	A RECAPITULATION	
1st subject	2nd subject	1st and/or 2nd subject	2nd subject	2nd subject

Step 2 – Chord sequence

On the next page, write the seven triads (I-VII) for your home key, using capital letters. Add *m* for minor and *dim* for diminished.

Now compose a 16-bar chord sequence for your first subject starting and ending with the tonic (I). There should be four phrases, each consisting of four bars. Use a strong progression from each bar to the next:

- Up a fourth
- Up a second
- Down a third
- Up a fifth

Each phrase should end with a cadence:

- Perfect V or vii to I
- Imperfect I, II or IV to V
- Interrupted V to VI
- Plagal IV to I

Chord sequence for First Subject

Chord (I-VII)	I	II	III	IV	V	VI	VII
in major keys	major	minor	minor	major	major	minor	diminished
in minor keys	minor	diminished	major	minor	major	major	diminished
Chord symbol							

I			
			I

Chord sequence for Second Subject (in Exposition)

Chord (I-VII)	I	II	III	IV	V	VI	VII
in major keys	major	minor	minor	major	major	minor	diminished
in minor keys	minor	diminished	major	minor	major	major	diminished
Chord symbol							

I			
			I

Step 3 – Left hand accompaniment

Convert your chord sequence into an accompanying pattern for the left hand by using a pattern chosen from the typical Classical-era accompaniments below, or similar. (These are all based on C major and 4/4 time signature, but they can be adapted to any chord or time signature.)

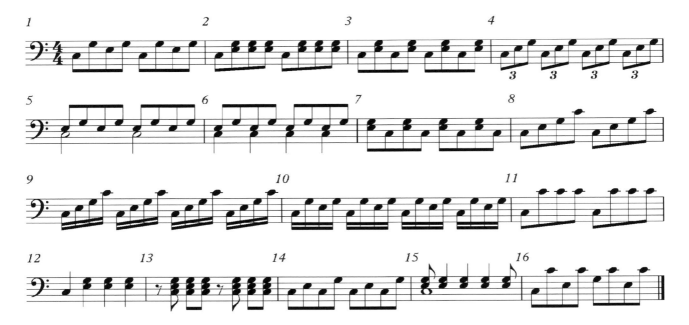

Step 4 – Melodic rhythm

Compose two different four-bar rhythms by starting with a short motif and extending/developing it. Use a longer note at the end of each phrase. (Each of the empty boxes below represents one bar.)

Rhythm 1				
Rhythm 2				

Step 5 - Composing the melody

Write a melody using the scale of your chosen key (e.g. C major). Bear in mind the following:

- The notes should be played easily on a piano without too many changes of hand position
- The range of the melody should be no more than an octave and a half
- Try to create a recognisable melodic shape over each four-bar phrase
- Begin and end each bar on chord notes
- Most of the melody should be stepwise (i.e. the notes are next to each other)
- Only leap between chord notes

Step 6 – Second subject

Repeat Steps 2-5 to create a different chord sequence, accompanying pattern and melody for your second subject. Don't forget that it will be in a different (but closely related) key.

Step 7 – Bridge passages

Compose a short section (2-4 bars long) which manages the transition between the first subject and second subject. Try adapting the melodic material of the first subject so it becomes more like the second subject.

- The bridge in the exposition should modulate (change key), so start on the tonic of the first subject, then use the dominant of the new key, then the tonic of the second subject.
- The bridge in the recapitulation should not modulate, so adapt the bridge section so it does not change key.

Step 8 – Coda/codetta

Compose another short section, this time using simple tonic and dominant harmony and a melody based on scales on arpeggios, to finish off the exposition. Extend it slightly to make an even more decisive end to the recapitulation and the whole piece.

Step 9 – Development section

This is where you can treat the first and/or second subject more freely, transforming the motifs, and using a variety of keys, textures and dynamics. Think of the development section as being a series of mini-variations on your themes from the exposition. You can transform the motifs (e.g. by inversion, retrograde, diminution, augmentation etc.). You may even wish to introduce new material (e.g. a countermelody). Write the keys you intend to use in your plan under Step 1.

Step 10 - Markings

Add the following markings to complete your score:-

- **Tempo** marking at the beginning of the score (right click > Text > Tempo > right click or type in)
- **Dynamics** at the beginning of the score, and possibly elsewhere (ctrl+E > right click or type in)
- **Phrasing** put a slur over each phrase of melody (click first bar of melody, shift+click last bar, press S) OR mark a more detached/staccato articulation
- **Title** at the top of the score (right click > Text > Title > type in)
- **Composer** your name at the top right of the score (right click > Composer > type in)
- **Date** at the top left of the score (right click > Lyricist > type in)

Beethoven's *Pathétique* Sonata

Attacca subito l' Allegro:

Beethoven's *Pathétique* Sonata: Structure and Tonality

Listen to the first movement of Beethoven's *Pathétique* Sonata with the score and complete the table below.

Overall structure: _____ form

Main section	Smaller section	Starts at bar	Key

Beethoven's *Pathétique* Sonata: other elements

Harmony

- Variety of cadences, for example:
    - bar 4.4-5.1 _____ cadence
    - bar 9.2-9.3 _____ cadence
    - bar 26-7 _____ cadence
- Variety of chords used, for example:
    - Bar 10.3 _____ inversion
    - Bar 10.4 _____(chord V) _____ (four-note chord)
- Bars 11-14 use a _____ (chord I) _____ (sustained/repeated note) in the bass
- Bars 167-187 use a _____ (chord V) _____ (sustained/repeated note) in the bass
- Bar 294: example of a _____ _____ (chord with four notes each separated by a minor third)

Melody and Accompaniment

- Bars 51-88: first second of the second subject alternates _____ (short, detached notes) and _____ (smooth, joined notes) motifs
- Bars 57-58: _____ (type of ornament) used in melody
- Bars 89-99: second section of second subject uses _____ bass (characteristic piano accompanying figure of the Classical Era)

Tonality

- Variety of keys used, including:
    - home key of _____
    - first section of second subject in _____
    - second section of second subject in _____
    - introduction of Development section in _____
    - fast section of Development section starts in _____
    - Recapitulation (bars 208.1-201.1) _____
    - Recapitulation (bars 211.2-214.2) _____
    - Recapitulation (bars 215.1-219.2) _____
    - Recapitulation (bars 215.1-219.2) _____

Rhythm

- Bars 139-143: beginning of fast section in Development uses an _____ (lengthened) version of the motif first heard in the Introduction

Mozart Sonata in C, K.545

Köchel Nr. 545

Appendices
Glossary

Melody

Scale – the notes used in a piece in pitch order. Degrees of the major or minor scale:

I tonic   II supertonic   III mediant   IV subdominant   V dominant   VI submediant   VII leading-note

Diatonic – in a major or minor key (as opposed to chromatic, modal or atonal)

Major – 'happy' scale made up of tone, tone, semitone, tone, tone, tone, semitone (e.g. CDEFGABC)

Minor – 'sad' scale which comes in three versions:

   Natural minor - tone, semitone, tone, tone, semitone, tone, tone (e.g. ABCDEFGA)

   Melodic minor – like natural minor but with sharpened 6th and 7th notes when ascending

   Harmonic minor – like natural minor but with sharpened 7th note

Chromatic(ism) – using accidentals not in the key signature

Tonal(ity) – describing whether a major/minor key or mode is used

Pentatonic – using five notes, e.g. CDEGA (pentatonic major) or ACDEG (pentatonic minor)

Atonal(ity) – not using a key at all

Mode/modal – similar to a scale, using a different combination of tones and semitones.

   Ionian – CDEFGABC (same as a major scale)
   Dorian – DEFGABCD
   Phrygian – EFGABCDE
   Lydian – FGABCDEF
   Mixolydian – GABCDEFG
   Aeolian – ABCDEFGA (same as a natural minor scale)
   Locrian - BCDEFGAB

Interval – the distance between two pitches (semitone, tone, second, third, fourth, fifth, sixth, seventh, octave). Seconds, thirds and sixth can be major or minor; fourths, fifths and octaves can be perfect. Any interval can be augmented (a semitone further away) or diminished (a semitone closer together).

Conjunct – a melody using mainly steps (next-door neighbour notes)

Disjunct – a melody using mainly leaps (notes that are not next to each other)

Passing note – a note in the melody that 'passes' between two chord notes

Pedal – a note that is sustained or repeated while the harmony changes (compare **drone**)

Portamento (Italian for 'carrying') – sliding from one pitch to another

Tonality & Harmony

Harmony – combination of different pitches to make different chords

Chords – two or more notes sounding together

Consonant/ce – notes that sound good together

Dissonant/ce – notes that sound bad or clash together

Triads – a three-note chord, which comes in four varieties:

Major triad: 4 semitones + 3 semitones (e.g. C E G)

Minor triad: 3 semitones + 4 semitones (e.g. C Eb G)

Diminished triad: 3 semitones + 3 semitones (e.g. C Eb Gb)

Augmented triad: 4 semitones + 4 semitones (e.g. C E G#)

Seventh chord – a triad plus a (usually minor) seventh above the root, e.g. C7 = C E G Bb

Extended chord – a seventh chord with an additional 9th, 11th or 13th above the root

Altered chord – a chord which contains note(s) a semitone higher or lower than those in the scale being used

Added note chord – a chord with some extra notes not in the basic chord, e.g. sus2 and sus4

Cadence - two chords to end a phrase or section:

Perfect (V or vii to I), imperfect (I, ii or IV to V), plagal (IV to I), interrupted (V to vi)

Modulation – the process of changing key, usually via a pivot chord common to both keys and the dominant of the new key

Instruments & voices

Families of Instruments and Voices

Strings – Violin, Viola, 'Cello (short for Violoncello), Double Bass, Harp

Woodwind – Flute (piccolo), Oboe (cor anglais), Clarinet (bass clarinet), Bassoon (contrabassoon)

Brass – French Horn, Trumpet, Trombone, Tuba

Percussion – Timpani, Bass Drum, Snare (or Side) Drum, Triangle, etc.

Keyboard – Piano, harpsichord, organ, synthesiser

Voices – Soprano (high female), Mezzo-soprano (medium female), (Contr)alto (low female), Countertenor or male alto (falsetto male), Tenor (high male), Baritone (medium male), Bass (low male)

Pop/rock/jazz instruments

Electric guitar – 6 strings tuned, from lowest to highest, EADGBE (see Buckley for techniques)

Bass guitar (sometimes called **Electric Bass**) – 4 strings, tuned the same as a double bass (EADG)

Drum kit – bass drum, snare drum, ride cymbal (for rhythms), crash cymbals (for effects), tom toms (two mounted and one floor tom), hi-hat (two cymbals clamped together)

Electric piano – e.g. Wurlitzer

Synthesiser - keyboard playing digital sounds and samples

Saxophone – single-reeded woodwind instrument with metal body (both alto and tenor saxophones feature in *All Blues*)

Folk/world instruments

Fiddle, Bodhran, Uilleann pipes, **Accordion, Bouzouki** – European folk instruments

Balaphone, Djembe, Mbira, Marimba, Kora, Talking Drum – African instruments

Sitar, Tabla, Bansuri, Esraj, Sarangi, Pakhawaj, Sarod, Finger cymbals – Indian instruments

Gongs (ageng, kempul, kenong), Metallophones (demung, saron, peking), Ciblon, Chengcheng – Indonesian gamelan

Instrumental and vocal effects

Vocables/vocalise – singing

Melisma(tic) – several notes to one syllable

Syllabic – one note to each syllable of text

Tremolo – rapidly repeated note (e.g. on a violin) or alternation between two notes (e.g. on a piano)

Portamento/slide - moving gradually from one pitch to another

Vibrato – effect adding slight fluctuation of pitch

Slide – moving left hand between frets while the string is still vibrating

Distortion - deliberately fuzzy sound as if the volume is turned up too high

Pizzicato – plucking (when applied to bowed strings) – **arco** means return to bowing

Studio effects

Sample – short section of recorded music

Delay/echo – digital effect which plays a sound again after a short delay

Reverb – complex digital effect which gives the impression of performing in a room or hall

EQ (equaliser) – technique of boosting certain frequencies (pitches) in the sound

Modulation (in this sense) – slight fluctuation of pitch

Texture

Monophonic - unaccompanied melody (could be performed by more than one person)

Homophonic - melody and chords

Polyphonic - several tunes at once

Heterophonic - variations of same tune played at the same time

Counterpoint/contrapuntal - several tunes at once

Imitation – one instrument/voice copies another (either afterwards or overlapping)

Canon – exact imitation of a motif or melody, overlapping with its first occurence

Layered – several independent parts performed together

Call-and-response – leader plays/sings something, others echo or give an 'answer'

Unison – a melody played or sung by two or more performers at the same pitch

Octaves – a melody played or sung by two or more performers an octave apart

Rhythm

Metre – the grouping of beats in bars:

>**Duple** – two beats in a bar

>**Triple** – three beats in a bar

>**Quadruple** – four beats in a bar

Time signature – the two numbers, one on top of the other, at the beginning of a piece or section of music indicating the metre. The top number indicates the number of beats per bar. The bottom number indicates what type of beat: usually 2 (minims), 4 (crotchets) or 8 (quavers).

Simple time – time signature where each beat divides into 2 or 4, e.g. 2/4, 3/4, 4/4, 2/2, 3/2

Compound time – time signature where each beat divides into 3, e.g. 6/8, 9/8, 12/8, 6/4

Free time – without sense of pulse

The following note-lengths are based on a crotchet beat (when 4 is the bottom number of the time signature):

>Semiquaver ♪ - ¼ of a beat (half the length of a quaver)

>Quaver ♪ - ½ a beat (half the length of a crotchet)

>Crotchet ♩ - 1 beat (half the length of a minim)

>Minim ♩ - 2 beats (half the length of a semibreve)

>Dotted minim ♩. – 3 beats (one and a half times the length of a minim)

>Semibreve ○ – 4 beats (length of two minims or four crotchets)

Dotted rhythms – a dot adds half the length of the original note

Triplets – three notes in the space of two

Syncopation – off-beat rhythm

Augmentation – rhythm or motif repeated with longer note values

Diminution – rhythm or motif repeated with shorter note values

Cross-rhythm – rhythms that are accented 'across' the metre, for example a hemiola (see below)

Hemiola – in triple time, a cross-rhythm of 3x2-beat notes (instead of 2x3-beat notes) in the lead-up to a cadence (particularly used in Baroque music)

Tempo

Presto – very fast

Vivace – fast, lively

Allegro – fast

Moderato – moderate pace

Andante – walking pace

Adagio - slow

bpm – beats per minute, e.g. 60bpm = 1 beat per second

Accelerando (accel.) – getting quicker

Ritardando (rit.) – getting slower

Rallentando (rall.) – getting slower

Rubato – literally 'robbed' time, where the tempo fluctuates slightly for expressive purposes

Pause/Fermata – held note or rest

Dynamics

ppp (very very quiet), **pp** (very quiet), **p** (quiet), **mp** (moderately quiet)

fff (very very loud), **ff** (very loud), **f** (loud), **mf** (moderately loud)

Crescendo (cresc.) – getting louder (<)

Diminuendo (dim.) – getting quieter (>)

Decrescendo (decresc.) – getting quieter

Sforzando (sfz) – heavily accented

Structure

Popular/folk music

Intro (introduction) – first section, usually before main melody begins

Verse – repeating section with different words each time

Chorus – repeating section, usually with same words each time, more of a climax than a verse

Middle 8 – section which contrasts with verse and chorus (not necessarily 8 bars long)

Bridge (**pre-chorus**) – section leading into chorus

Link – short section joining one section to another

Outro – final section

Classical music

Binary form – two contrasting sections (AB)

Ternary form – repeated section with contrasting middle section (ABA)

Rondo form – initial section recurs after alternating with different sections (ABACA)

Sonata form – large-scale ternary form where the outer sections (**exposition** and **recapitulation**) are in binary form (AB) and the middle section (**development**) uses parts of both A and B

Theme and variations – Melody which reappears in different versions (A A_1 A_2 A_3 etc.)

Ostinato - a short repeating rhythmic/melodic pattern

Riff - a short repeating melodic pattern, usually syncopated and particularly in popular music

Coda – final section

Wider Listening Record

Title	Composer
Genre	Period

Dynamics

From loud (forte) to soft (piano)

Getting louder (crescendo) – getting softer (diminuendo)

Articulation: accent, legato, staccato, marcato

Rhythm, Metre, Tempo

Semibreve, minim, crotchet, etc., dotted rhythms, syncopation, hemiola, cross-rhythms, duplets, triplets, etc. Duple, triple, quadruple simple, compound time

Allegro, adagio, accelerando, ritardando, rubato, pause

Tonality

Major, minor, atonal, modal

Structure

Binary, ternary, variations, strophic, sonata form, AABA

Melody

Major, minor, atonal, modal, pentatonic

Conjunct, disjunct, shape, range

Non-harmonic notes: passing, auxiliary, etc.

Instrumentation, Timbre, Sonority

Voices: soprano, alto, tenor, bass, SATB choir

Woodwind: flute, oboe, clarinet, bassoon,

Brass: horn, trumpet, trombone, tuba

Strings: violin, viola, cello, double bass, harp, guitar

Percussion: timpani, drum kit, bass drum

Keyboards: piano, harpsichord, synthesiser, organ,

Studio effects, mute, pizzicato, harmonics

Texture

Monophonic, (melody dominant) homophonic, polyphonic, heterophonic, imitation, call-and-response

Harmony

Major/minor/augmented/diminished triads, inversions

Tonic, supertonic, mediant, subdominant, dominant, submediant, leading note, sevenths, chord progressions, cadences, modulation

ABCDE: Applied chords, Borrowed chords, Chromatic sixths, Diminished sevenths, Extended chords

Wider Listening Record

Title	Composer
Genre	Period

Dynamics

From loud (forte) to soft (piano)
Getting louder (crescendo) – getting softer (diminuendo)
Articulation: accent, legato, staccato, marcato

Rhythm, Metre, Tempo

Semibreve, minim, crotchet, etc., dotted rhythms, syncopation, hemiola, cross-rhythms, duplets, triplets, etc. Duple, triple, quadruple simple, compound time
Allegro, adagio, accelerando, ritardando, rubato, pause

Tonality

Major, minor, atonal, modal

Structure

Binary, ternary, variations, strophic, sonata form, AABA

Melody

Major, minor, atonal, modal, pentatonic
Conjunct, disjunct, shape, range
Non-harmonic notes: passing, auxiliary, etc.

Instrumentation, Timbre, Sonority

Voices: soprano, alto, tenor, bass, SATB choir
Woodwind: flute, oboe, clarinet, bassoon,
Brass: horn, trumpet, trombone, tuba
Strings: violin, viola, cello, double bass, harp, guitar
Percussion: timpani, drum kit, bass drum
Keyboards: piano, harpsichord, synthesiser, organ,
Studio effects, mute, pizzicato, harmonics

Texture

Monophonic, (melody dominant) homophonic, polyphonic, heterophonic, imitation, call-and-response

Harmony

Major/minor/augmented/diminished triads, inversions
Tonic, supertonic, mediant, subdominant, dominant, submediant, leading note, sevenths, chord progressions, cadences, modulation
ABCDE: Applied chords, Borrowed chords, Chromatic sixths, Diminished sevenths, Extended chords

Wider Listening Record

Title	Composer
Genre	Period

Dynamics

From loud (forte) to soft (piano)
Getting louder (crescendo) – getting softer (diminuendo)
Articulation: accent, legato, staccato, marcato

Rhythm, Metre, Tempo

Semibreve, minim, crotchet, etc., dotted rhythms, syncopation, hemiola, cross-rhythms, duplets, triplets, etc. Duple, triple, quadruple simple, compound time
Allegro, adagio, accelerando, ritardando, rubato, pause

Tonality

Major, minor, atonal, modal

Structure

Binary, ternary, variations, strophic, sonata form, AABA

Melody

Major, minor, atonal, modal, pentatonic
Conjunct, disjunct, shape, range
Non-harmonic notes: passing, auxiliary, etc.

Instrumentation, Timbre, Sonority

Voices: soprano, alto, tenor, bass, SATB choir
Woodwind: flute, oboe, clarinet, bassoon,
Brass: horn, trumpet, trombone, tuba
Strings: violin, viola, cello, double bass, harp, guitar
Percussion: timpani, drum kit, bass drum
Keyboards: piano, harpsichord, synthesiser, organ,
Studio effects, mute, pizzicato, harmonics

Texture

Monophonic, (melody dominant) homophonic, polyphonic, heterophonic, imitation, call-and-response

Harmony

Major/minor/augmented/diminished triads, inversions
Tonic, supertonic, mediant, subdominant, dominant, submediant, leading note, sevenths, chord progressions, cadences, modulation
ABCDE: Applied chords, Borrowed chords, Chromatic sixths, Diminished sevenths, Extended chords

Wider Listening Record

Title	Composer
Genre	**Period**

Dynamics

From loud (forte) to soft (piano)
Getting louder (crescendo) – getting softer (diminuendo)
Articulation: accent, legato, staccato, marcato

Rhythm, Metre, Tempo

Semibreve, minim, crotchet, etc., dotted rhythms, syncopation, hemiola, cross-rhythms, duplets, triplets, etc. Duple, triple, quadruple simple, compound time
Allegro, adagio, accelerando, ritardando, rubato, pause

Tonality

Major, minor, atonal, modal

Structure

Binary, ternary, variations, strophic, sonata form, AABA

Melody

Major, minor, atonal, modal, pentatonic
Conjunct, disjunct, shape, range
Non-harmonic notes: passing, auxiliary, etc.

Instrumentation, Timbre, Sonority

Voices: soprano, alto, tenor, bass, SATB choir
Woodwind: flute, oboe, clarinet, bassoon,
Brass: horn, trumpet, trombone, tuba
Strings: violin, viola, cello, double bass, harp, guitar
Percussion: timpani, drum kit, bass drum
Keyboards: piano, harpsichord, synthesiser, organ,
Studio effects, mute, pizzicato, harmonics

Texture

Monophonic, (melody dominant) homophonic, polyphonic, heterophonic, imitation, call-and-response

Harmony

Major/minor/augmented/diminished triads, inversions
Tonic, supertonic, mediant, subdominant, dominant, submediant, leading note, sevenths, chord progressions, cadences, modulation
ABCDE: Applied chords, Borrowed chords, Chromatic sixths, Diminished sevenths, Extended chords

Wider Listening Record

Title		Composer	
Genre		Period	

Dynamics

From loud (forte) to soft (piano)
Getting louder (crescendo) – getting softer (diminuendo)
Articulation: accent, legato, staccato, marcato

Rhythm, Metre, Tempo

Semibreve, minim, crotchet, etc., dotted rhythms, syncopation, hemiola, cross-rhythms, duplets, triplets, etc. Duple, triple, quadruple simple, compound time
Allegro, adagio, accelerando, ritardando, rubato, pause

Tonality

Major, minor, atonal, modal

Structure

Binary, ternary, variations, strophic, sonata form, AABA

Melody

Major, minor, atonal, modal, pentatonic
Conjunt, disjunct, shape, range
Non-harmonic notes: passing, auxiliary, etc.

Instrumentation, Timbre, Sonority

Voices: soprano, alto, tenor, bass, SATB choir
Woodwind: flute, oboe, clarinet, bassoon,
Brass: horn, trumpet, trombone, tuba
Strings: violin, viola, cello, double bass, harp, guitar
Percussion: timpani, drum kit, bass drum
Keyboards: piano, harpsichord, synthesiser, organ,
Studio effects, mute, pizzicato, harmonics

Texture

Monophonic, (melody dominant) homophonic, polyphonic, heterophonic, imitation, call-and-response

Harmony

Major/minor/augmented/diminished triads, inversions
Tonic, supertonic, mediant, subdominant, dominant, submediant, leading note, sevenths, chord progressions, cadences, modulation
ABCDE: Applied chords, Borrowed chords, Chromatic sixths, Diminished sevenths, Extended chords

Wider Listening Record

Title	Composer
Genre	Period

Dynamics
From loud (forte) to soft (piano)
Getting louder (crescendo) – getting softer (diminuendo)
Articulation: accent, legato, staccato, marcato

Rhythm, Metre, Tempo
Semibreve, minim, crotchet, etc., dotted rhythms, syncopation, hemiola, cross-rhythms, duplets, triplets, etc. Duple, triple, quadruple simple, compound time
Allegro, adagio, accelerando, ritardando, rubato, pause

Tonality
Major, minor, atonal, modal

Structure
Binary, ternary, variations, strophic, sonata form, AABA

Melody
Major, minor, atonal, modal, pentatonic
Conjunct, disjunct, shape, range
Non-harmonic notes: passing, auxiliary, etc.

Instrumentation, Timbre, Sonority
Voices: soprano, alto, tenor, bass, SATB choir
Woodwind: flute, oboe, clarinet, bassoon,
Brass: horn, trumpet, trombone, tuba
Strings: violin, viola, cello, double bass, harp, guitar
Percussion: timpani, drum kit, bass drum
Keyboards: piano, harpsichord, synthesiser, organ,
Studio effects, mute, pizzicato, harmonics

Texture
Monophonic, (melody dominant) homophonic, polyphonic, heterophonic, imitation, call-and-response

Harmony
Major/minor/augmented/diminished triads, inversions
Tonic, supertonic, mediant, subdominant, dominant, submediant, leading note, sevenths, chord progressions, cadences, modulation
ABCDE: Applied chords, Borrowed chords, Chromatic sixths, Diminished sevenths, Extended chords

Performing assessment form (1)

Pupil ....

Instrument...

Title of piece...

Composer...

Solo / Ensemble *(circle as appropriate)*

No.	Criterion	Mark	Max.
1	Technical control		8
2	Expression and interpretation		8
3	Accuracy and fluency		8
	Level of difficulty (see scaling grid below) LD (less difficult), S (standard) or MD (more difficult)	LD S MD *(circle as appropriate)*	
	TOTAL		30

Teacher's notes	Raw mark	Less difficult *(below grade 4)*	Standard *(grade 4)*	More difficult *(above grade 4)*
	1	1	1	2
	2	2	3	3
	3	3	4	4
	4	4	5	6
	5	5	6	8
	6	6	8	9
	7	7	9	11
	8	8	10	12
	9	9	11	14
	10	10	13	15
	11	11	14	17
	12	12	15	18
	13	13	16	20
	14	14	18	21
	15	15	19	23
	16	16	20	24
	17	17	21	26
	18	18	23	27
	19	19	24	29
	20	20	25	30
	21	21	26	30
	22	22	28	30
	23	23	29	30
	24	24	30	30

Performing assessment form (2)

Pupil ....

Instrument...

Title of piece...

Composer..

Solo / Ensemble *(circle as appropriate)*

No.	Criterion	Mark	Max.
1	Technical control		8
2	Expression and interpretation		8
3	Accuracy and fluency		8
	Level of difficulty (see scaling grid below) LD (less difficult), S (standard) or MD (more difficult)	LD S MD *(circle as appropriate)*	
	TOTAL		30

Teacher's notes	Raw mark	Less difficult *(below grade 4)*	Standard *(grade 4)*	More difficult *(above grade 4)*
	1	1	1	2
	2	2	3	3
	3	3	4	4
	4	4	5	6
	5	5	6	8
	6	6	8	9
	7	7	9	11
	8	8	10	12
	9	9	11	14
	10	10	13	15
	11	11	14	17
	12	12	15	18
	13	13	16	20
	14	14	18	21
	15	15	19	23
	16	16	20	24
	17	17	21	26
	18	18	23	27
	19	19	24	29
	20	20	25	30
	21	21	26	30
	22	22	28	30
	23	23	29	30
	24	24	30	30

Performing assessment form (3)

Pupil ....

Instrument...

Title of piece...

Composer...

Solo / Ensemble *(circle as appropriate)*

No.	Criterion	Mark	Max.
1	Technical control		8
2	Expression and interpretation		8
3	Accuracy and fluency		8
	Level of difficulty (see scaling grid below) LD (less difficult), S (standard) or MD (more difficult)	LD S MD *(circle as appropriate)*	
	TOTAL		30

Teacher's notes	Raw mark	Less difficult *(below grade 4)*	Standard *(grade 4)*	More difficult *(above grade 4)*
	1	1	1	2
	2	2	3	3
	3	3	4	4
	4	4	5	6
	5	5	6	8
	6	6	8	9
	7	7	9	11
	8	8	10	12
	9	9	11	14
	10	10	13	15
	11	11	14	17
	12	12	15	18
	13	13	16	20
	14	14	18	21
	15	15	19	23
	16	16	20	24
	17	17	21	26
	18	18	23	27
	19	19	24	29
	20	20	25	30
	21	21	26	30
	22	22	28	30
	23	23	29	30
	24	24	30	30

Performing assessment form (4)

Pupil ....

Instrument...

Title of piece...

Composer...

Solo / Ensemble (*circle as appropriate*)

No.	Criterion	Mark	Max.
1	Technical control		8
2	Expression and interpretation		8
3	Accuracy and fluency		8
	Level of difficulty (see scaling grid below) LD (less difficult), S (standard) or MD (more difficult)	LD S MD (circle as appropriate)	
	TOTAL		30

Teacher's notes	Raw mark	Less difficult (*below grade 4*)	Standard (*grade 4*)	More difficult (*above grade 4*)
	1	1	1	2
	2	2	3	3
	3	3	4	4
	4	4	5	6
	5	5	6	8
	6	6	8	9
	7	7	9	11
	8	8	10	12
	9	9	11	14
	10	10	13	15
	11	11	14	17
	12	12	15	18
	13	13	16	20
	14	14	18	21
	15	15	19	23
	16	16	20	24
	17	17	21	26
	18	18	23	27
	19	19	24	29
	20	20	25	30
	21	21	26	30
	22	22	28	30
	23	23	29	30
	24	24	30	30

Composing assessment form (1)

Pupil .... **Date**...............................

Title of piece...

Brief/purpose..

Free composition / Area of Study 1 2 3 4 *(circle as appropriate)*

No.	Criterion	Mark	Max.
1	Developing musical ideas		10
2	Demonstrating technical control		10
3	Composing with musical coherence		10
	TOTAL		30

Teacher's notes

Composing assessment form (2)

Pupil .... **Date**............................

Title of piece..

Brief/purpose...

Free composition / Area of Study 1 2 3 4 *(circle as appropriate)*

No.	Criterion	Mark	Max.
1	Developing musical ideas		10
2	Demonstrating technical control		10
3	Composing with musical coherence		10
	TOTAL		30

Teacher's notes

Composing assessment form (3)

Pupil .... **Date**..........................

Title of piece..

Brief/purpose...

Free composition / Area of Study 1 2 3 4 *(circle as appropriate)*

No.	Criterion	Mark	Max.
1	Developing musical ideas		10
2	Demonstrating technical control		10
3	Composing with musical coherence		10
	TOTAL		30

Teacher's notes

Composing assessment form (4)

Pupil .... **Date**..............................

Title of piece...

Brief/purpose..

Free composition / Area of Study 1 2 3 4 *(circle as appropriate)*

No.	Criterion	Mark	Max.
1	Developing musical ideas		10
2	Demonstrating technical control		10
3	Composing with musical coherence		10
	TOTAL		30

Teacher's notes

Acknowledgements

All images and music typesetting © the author, except:

Page 9: The *Wicked* marquee on the Ford/Oriental Theater in Chicago by bradleypjohnson (Creative Commons Licence) https://commons.wikimedia.org/wiki/File:Wicked,_oriental_theater_in_chicago.jpg

Page 10: Decisive moment in the high school musical *Oklahoma!* by woodleywonderworks bradleypjohnson (Creative Commons Licence) https://www.flickr.com/photos/wwworks/8566466403

Page 14: The Sound of Music: The front doors of the London Palladium on Argyll Street by Stephen McKay (Creative Commons Licence) https://commons.wikimedia.org/wiki/File:The_Sound_of_Music_-_geograph.org.uk_-_1129470.jpg

Page 15: The Shark girls extol the virtues of America in Portland Center Stage's production of *West Side Story* by Owen Carey (Public Domain) https://commons.wikimedia.org/wiki/File:The_Shark_girls_extol_the_virtues_of_America.jpg

Page 35: Publicity photo of Queen by Electra Records (Public Domain) https://commons.wikimedia.org/wiki/File:Queen_1976.JPG

Page 36: O rubor sanguinis by Hildergard of Bingen, c.1150 (Public Domain) https://www.youtube.com/watch?v=WDeR9MeGNPg

Page 52: Bill Haley and the Comets by Decca Records (Public Domain) https://commons.wikimedia.org/wiki/File:Bill_Haley_and_the_Comets1956.jpg

Page 54: The Beatles (unattributed, Public Domain) https://commons.wikimedia.org/wiki/File:Beatles_ad_1965_just_the_beatles_crop.jpg

Page 54: Electric guitar (unattributed, Creative Commons Licence) https://pixabay.com/en/electric-guitar-instrument-2022646/

Page 54: Bass guitar (unattributed, Creative Commons Licence) https://pixabay.com/en/bass-guitar-electric-guitar-axe-ax-155468/

Page 59: Esperanza Spalding - Concerto del 15 luglio 2009 a Fiesole – Firenze by Andrea Mancini (Creative Commons Licence) https://www.flickr.com/photos/pennello/3739998893

Page 71: Portrait of Ludwig van Beethoven composing the *Missa Solemnis* by Joseph Karl Stieler (Public Domain) https://commons.wikimedia.org/wiki/File:Beethoven.jpg

Pages 75-87: Bach's Brandenburg Concerto No. 5, edited by Wilhelm Rust (1822–1892) (Bach-Gesellschaft Ausgabe, Band 19, Leipzig: Breitkopf und Härtel, 1871, Public Domain) http://petrucci.mus.auth.gr/imglnks/usimg/f/f1/IMSLP272348-PMLP82083-Bach_-_Brandenburg_No.5_Dover_optimized.pdf

Page 91: Muzio Clemnti's Sonata in C (Schirmer edition (1904), Public Domain) https://imslp.nl/imglnks/usimg/b/b5/IMSLP29868-PMLP06617-Clementi_Op36_Schirmer.pdf

Pages 96-104: Beethoven's *Pathétique* Sonata, edited by Heinrich Schenker (1868–1935) (Vienna, Universal Edition, 1918-21, Public Domain) http://petrucci.mus.auth.gr/imglnks/usimg/c/c8/IMSLP00008-Beethoven,_L.v._-_Piano_Sonata_08.pdf

Pages 107-110: Mozart's Sonata in C, K.545, Peters Edition (1938), Public Domain https://imslp.nl/imglnks/usimg/2/2f/IMSLP70214-PMLP01855-KV_545.pdf

Printed in Great Britain
by Amazon